AMERICA'S
SECRET
CHILDREN'S
PRISONS

AMERICA'S SECRET CHILDREN'S PRISONS

WILLIAM D. ANDREWS

Trafford rev. 01/28/2011

 www.trafford.com

North America & International
toll-free: 1 888 232 4444 (USA & Canada)
phone: 250 383 6864 ♦ fax: 812 355 4082

America's Secret Children's Prisons
By William D. Andrews
A LOOK INSIDE FOSTER HOMES

Aspirins have proven very effective to stop headaches and sometimes help during heart attacks. Foster Homes and Out Of Home Placement have been portrayed as two of the best things that could happen for some children. After looking inside through this peek a boo glass,?" you will agree that an aspirin will not be enough. You will see why over forty percent in some areas end up in adult prisons? You will see why children are not allowed to talk to their parents or outsiders about life inside. Allow a child to talk and parents would know their children were being freely abused physically, verbally and sexually inside the system. Violence, racism, alcohol and drugs are common within the System. What would a parent feel or do if this knowledge was known? A wall of protective silence has been built around The Human Resource System. This has allowed the unspeakable to occur inside the system. Some of which would put those of us on the outside into prison for life. Remove the silence. What would a parent think or do if he or she knew this was being done with the knowledge and often the consent of the System Directors? What would America think if we found a parent accused, humiliated, Defiled, and made a criminal through the courts in order to give his or her children to waiting adopters? Who would dream that prostitution is being promoted within the system? Could we believe some of our girls today are being used as sex slaves? Would you be shocked to find that at times the only oversight is System Personnel themselves? Who Oversees Them? It has been a shocking thirty-five year Experience for William D. Andrews in working with Out Of Home persons. Over 60 percent of the children removed from homes in some states are listed as unwarranted removals. This means taking your children from your home is usually not justified. Read and believe. See America's future by looking at it's past and present. Can a Foster Home or Out Of Home Placement really become a prison?

About The Author

Thirty years a\go, social workers, statement that if a parent is moved out of the home, we can give them aid, sparked his parent and children's advocacy. William D. Andrews
Was bon in Gates, Pennsylvania? One of seventeen children living in a rundown house. Yet his mother still had enough to share with so many others.

After graduating from high school, William became a minister and traveled extensively, emphasizing the training of preachers. His love and compassion for the poor, hopeless, mistreated, hungry and homeless involved him in countless efforts of help and counseling. He considers himself a servant.

CONTENTS

ACKNOWLEDGEMENTS

DUE TO THE PERSONAL CONCERNS AND FEARS OF MANY OF THOSE THAT SUPPLIED THEIR STORIES, ADVICE RESEARCH AND INFORMATION, MY RECOGNISTION IS WITHOUTS PERSONAL NAMES.

I DO GIVE THANKS TO ATTORNEYS, COURT EMPLOYEES, PROBATION PERSONS, EX MILITARY, PRISON HELP ORGANIZATIONS, ADOPTION AGENCIES, SEVERAL REHAB ORGANIZATIONS, CRIME PREVENTION GROUPS, YOUTH GROUPS, GANG RELATED GROUPS, DRUG RELATED GROUPS, ALCOHOL RELATED GROUPS, HOMELESS RELATED GROUPS, FAMILY RELATED GROUPS, INMATES AND FORMER INMATES OF PRISONS, AND OUT OF HOME PLACEMENTS, WELFARE PERSONNEL, SCHOOL PERSONNEL, JUVENILE RELATED GROUPS, POLITICAL PERSONS INCLUDING ELECTED OFFICIALS, CIVIL RIGHTS GROUPS, AND CIVIL RIGHTS ACTIVISTS, POLICE PERSONNEL AND SEVERAL LIBRARIES AND THE MANY INDIVIDUALS DEDICATED TO YOUTH, FAMILY, HONESTY, JUSTICE AND FAIRNESS IN OUR NATION.

VERIFICATION OF VARIOUS LAWS AND PRACTICE IS EXTREMELY VITAL TO THE PROTECTION OF AMERICA'S FREE NATION STATUS. INDIVIDUALS ARE OFTEN

INTIMIDATED BUT KNOWLEDGE IS MORE WIDE SPREAD THAN SOME WOULD BE INCLINED TO BELIEVE. THANKS FOR VERIFICATION. NOW LET OUR NATION BE INCLINED TO BELIEVE, NOW LET OUR NATION PRAY FOR COMPLIANCE THAT OUR GREATNESS SHALL CONTINUE AND EXCEL.

SPECIAL MENTION TO THE STATES OF CALIFORNIA, COLORADO, FLORIDA, IOWA, ILLINOIS, NEW JERSEY, NEW YORK, MISSISSIPPI, WASHINGTON, MISSOURI AND THEIR RESIDENTS.

I AM FOREVER INDEBTED TO THE CHURCH FAMILIES THAT PRAYED FOR ME. PRAYER HAS BEEN A WALL BETWEEN MYSELF AND THREATS OF FINES, JAIL, LIFE IMPRISONMENT, DEATH THREATS, VIOLENCE AND OTHER INTIMIDATIONS FOR MYSELF AND SOME THAT HELPED ME AS I GATHERED AND SPOKE TRUTH AND FACTS. MAY THIS BOOK BE A LIFE CHANGER FOR SOME?

DEDICATED TO

MIA, LAUREN, CANDACE, ALEX, TYRESE, (ELI)

FOSTER CARE ROCK ** MY SONG OF DEDICATION **
VARIOUS MELODIES

HELLO AMERICA I'M A CHILD ON THE RUN.
I DIDN'T KILL ANYBODY AND I DIDN'T STEAL.
RUNNING FROM THE LAW AINT NO FUN,
BUT BELIEVE ME, MY RUNNING IS REAL.

I'M RUNNING HOME AND THAT'S GOOD NEWS.
I'M RUNNING FROM FOSTER CARE.
I WAS LIED TO AND SEXUALLY ABUSED,
HANDS WERE LAID ON ME AND I RAN FROM THERE.

I WANTED TO BE AN ARTIST AND PLAY A GUITAR,
MY DAD SAID GREAT, YOU WILL GO VERY FAR.
FOSTER CARE CAME AND TOOK ME FROM MY HOME.
I HAD MY OWN BUSINESS AT AGE 14. FOSTER CARE SAID
LEAVE IT ALONE.

MY DAD CAME TO RESCUE ME.
HE NEVER DRANK OR SMOKED, A KIND GENTLE MAN.
I WAS IN A FOSTER CARE PRISON. I WAS NOT FREE.
THEY LIED, SAID HE WAS OLD, MIGHT GET SICK. HE
DIDN'T FIT THEIR PLAN.

I AM RUNNING AWAY BUT I AM RUNNING HOME.

AINT GOT NO PHONE AND I AM ALL-ALONE.
POLICE CANT KEEP ME FROM MY FAMILY NOW.
I'M GONNA GET HOME, SOME WAY SOME HOW.

I BEEN PHYSICALLY ABUSED AND CALLED BAD NAMES.
FOSTER CARE PLAYED THOSE WICKED GAMES.
I WASN'T ALLOWED TO SEE MY SISTER OR BROTHERS,
COULDN'T EVEN CALL MY DAD OR MY MOTHER.

I WAS CURSED BY FOSTER PARENTS AND ASSAULTED BY
THEIR KIDS.
SOCIAL WORKERS WOULDN'T LISTEN, SAID IT WAS
LYING FIBS.
I CLIMBED OUT THE WINDOW AND AM RUNNING AWAY.
I'M GONNA FIND MY FAMILY AND WITH THEM I WILL
STAY.

I NEVER KNEW LIFE COULD BE SO SAD.
POLICE ARE CHASINGME AND I AINT EVEN BAD.
ALL I'M TRYING TO DO IS GET HOME TO MOM AND
DAD.
I'M ON THE RUN CAUSE I DON'T BELONG IN A FOSTER
CARE PAD.

I HAD TO SNEAK TO WRITE LETTERS AND HIDE TO
MAKE CALLS.
THEY TOLD LIES ON THE FAMILY TO BREAK MY WIIL.
I AM STILL RUNNING HOME TO MY FAMILLY. I WON'T
STUMBLE OR FALL.
BLOOD OVER RULES LIES. THAT IS MY FAMILY STILL.

RUN, RUN, RUN, FOR HOME.
RUN, RUN, RUN, FOR SISTER. RUN, RUN, RUN, FOR
BROTHER,
RUN, RUN, RUN, FOR DAD, RUN, RUN, AND RUN, FOR
MOTHER.
I'M RUNNING HOME FROM FOSTER CARE.

The Smuggled Letters of the Secret Conversations from Foster Care to Home

******** *wrote:*

From ; **** 2006**
Thank u *** When I get a**
chance I'll call u. But right
now all I can do is write. I
don't have much time so I'll
try 2 write u when I get a
chance cuzBC they watch me
like a hawk. Pray 4 me please.
I love you. And tell dad that I
love him 2. ok?

FROM: I'M THE QUEEN

DON'T EVEN TRIP. I GOT
YOU. REMEMBER OURS
TOO.

FEEL YOU, CHICK. I WON'T TELL NO ONE ABOUT NOTHING. I WAS just TELLING **** don't ever let no one keep you from us, okay? Just remember that no one can take what's in your mind. Keep us in your memories and in your thoughts and always remember that we're here for you. Don't act like you don't know how to be slick about your business. My email is **** ****

Don't act like you don't know how to do what it is you need to do we're family, kid. We're blood. Always remember that. We got the

same blood flowing in our veins and no one can take that away from us and no one can keep you guys from talking to us. It ain't no thang, kid. Just remember that we're always here for you. They're tryna break off all contact from us to you guys. I don't want to tell you guys this on the phone, so I'm letting you know on here. Make sure no one finds this, okay? And make sure you tell the boys. I'm gonna write **** an email, but someone might be reading his email, so just in case, I'm trusting you guys to give both him and ****that information and make sure they know and remember it. Cause they're tryna cut off all contact so that dad n I don't talk to any of you kids at all. And don't say nothing about it cause they'll let you guys know soon enough. Always remember to think before you act. Think about everything before you do anything and especially before you say anything, okay? I love you, kid. Remember that there's always a way to contact us. No one can take you guys out of our hearts. You be good and stay up, okay? Don't forget. I love you. Dad sends his love to both of you

Love always ****wrote

Dang girl you is good I miss you and dad so much they told me and**** that mom and dad were going to lose custody of us. They said that they haven't set up a court date yet but they're going to. Is dad there with you? Make sure he's reading this with you ok? Are you guys going to come down here for that? *****Is taking it pretty hard and we haven't talked to the boys yet to see if they know but its hard. Everything has been going all-wrong. I don't know how to react. It just hasn't hit me yet. I try so hard not to think about it but it's hard and I don't want to put stress on anybody so I hold it all inside. It's hard not being able to see the ones I love most and the family wasn't even trying to get us back. That's what hurts the most because the family should have been the first to be there. It makes me so mad because when they needed us we were there. Nobody else. Just us: our family. The only people who were trying to get us back were you, dad and mom. But it's so hard looking at my family. They don't even deserve to be called family! Help me **** I need somebody to talk to. It's so hard. I don't know what to do. I feel all alone right now. I'm so upset, so hurt. I can't even write good because I can't stop crying. I miss you guys so much. I need my family back. I don't want to be separated from anybody I love. Why, why did it have to be like this? Why? Why? Why? why? Dang, I can't do this on my own. I need somebody by my side! It hurts so bad to know that you all are gone. Gone out of my life. I need some support. I need somebody to cry with. Please don't make me go through losing my family alone. I love my dad I love my mom. I love my brothers and sister. I want to go home. I don't want to feel this pain anymore. Everybody who told me that they would always be there are all gone. They all lied. I miss my daddy so much. I miss you. I don't know how to handle a situation like this. I feel all alone. They all lied. ****On you dad everybody. I can't trust anybody. Why would God allow something like this to happen? Why? What did I do? What did we do to deserve this? I'm full of so much anger I don't know what to say or do. Who will take care of my family my brothers and sisters? One's already getting adopted. My baby brother who I love so much. It hurts me to see him calling somebody else mama and dada. But all I can do is bite my tongue. What do I do? Who do I talk to about the way I feel? They don't care. Nobody does! Sometimes I feel like shit and it makes me want to quit. Sometimes I feel is my life is really worth all this DRAMA? Don't get upset, I just really need to let it all out. I have been holding it in 4 so long. I just had to let it all out. I miss you guys so much. I miss having fun. I miss spending time with you and dad. I miss spending time with my family. I don't know what to say. When I ask them why can't I go with dad they tell me because dad's not cooperating. They tell me that dad doesn't want them 2 talk to his other children. Why dad can't you see that I am hurting? I am so hurt right now. I can't believe that my own family! My own family! let me down! All of it was lies. All lies. I don't know what to say! I hope your reading this dad cause I really need you right now! I need some kind of support! I am filled with so much anger that I have lost faith in God! I have 4gotten how to pray! I don't know why! I need to. I been praying for so long but this was not the result that I wanted. And yes dad all that you heard about me is true. I am not a virgin. And yes It hurts me so much everyday. Every time I hear your voice, something makes me want to break down in tears because I feel that I let you down. I have so much stuff that I want to tell you dad. I only trust you and I don't know why. After all you put us through, I still trust only you. It seems that this is the only way I can get my feelings out to you. I need you right now dad. I need somebody right now. I don't want to go out and be like my mom but it's hard to say no.

But every time I talk to you dad; something tells me not to give up because daddy wont let anything happen. Daddy won't let them take me away. Daddy will get us back. I love you so much dad. If you only knew what I'm feeling right now you would understand dad. I'm so, so sorry for letting you down. I really am and I am so sorry ****for everything I have ever done or ever said to you. I really am and no I am not drunk. I am fine. I just really needed to let my feelings out and cry a little bit. If mom only knew what we were and are going through she wouldn't be acting stupid. I am so, so sorry for letting you all down. I thought that I would make it through this letter without any tears but I guess I couldn't and **** and dad I really do love you! And dad don't worry about me. I will try to make it through even though it's hard. I just really want to see you guys. My heart yearns for my family back! And don't get scared I know that I sound like I'm going to hurt myself. Don't worry I'm not. I just really miss my loved ones and when they told me that you and mom were loosing parental rights, It hit me really hard. I will let you go now. I really do love you guys. I am just really frustrated and **** that poem that you wrote 4 us, it was really good. It made me cry. I just had to talk to somebody about my feelings because I keep it all bottled in and it hurts even more. I really do miss you guys. You don't even know and I have done some stupid things in my life and dad you are my best friend. Nobody ever knew that you were my best friend and I love you even more for that. I will try to learn from my mistakes in life and I'm sorry I let you down. You to **** well I will let you go now I do need some comfort thank you so much.

With love Your little sugar plum and your baby sister
P.S. I'm sorry for cursing and saying mean things with all my love.

SISTER wrote:

Oh honey! My dear, sweet baby sister, I don't want you to hurt the way you are. I'm so sorry, baby, that you are hurting like this. We're all missing you guys; we're all hurting, too. This is what I didn't want to hear, this is what made it so hard for me to think of you guys some times, thinking that you guys are hurting, too. I just want to take all the pain away from you guys. Don't you worry, baby girl, don't you worry at all. We are cooperating, we ARE trying to get you guys back, we are trying so hard to get you guys back. We don't want to let you guys down, honey. You guys are our family, our blood, our lives. I know it's hard, baby girl, just stay strong for us. God never gives us anything we can't handle, and you can handle this. You are strong. Be strong and don't give up. Don't let them win, **** We're going to be there when they try to do that, but they won't have you guys. They won't win, ****. I know it's hard, I know some times you feel like giving up, I know some times you lose faith in God, I understand, believe me, I understand how it feels to lose faith, to be angry, to feel like God doesn't care. Sweetheart, don't give up on us. We're fighting for you guys, we're fighting so hard. I know it must be hard seeing **** growing up with those people, but it's not yours or his fault. I know it hurts, baby girl, I'm so sorry. I just wish I could take every thing away and be there for you, right next to you and **** and **** and **** and little ****. We're gonna get through this. Remember what I told you, nothing and no one can take you guys away from us, nothing can take us out of your hearts or you out of ours. Just yesterday, Sister **** **** sent dad a CD of some songs that God had specifically touched her heart about concerning our family. In those songs, God told us that He knows the plan He has for us, and He'll give us Hope for tomorrow, joy for our sorrows, and strength for everything we go through. He also said it was a new season and that He'll bless us more than we could ever ask for. Honey, when you have no one to turn to, when no one seems to care, when no one's there and you're feeling all alone, just turn to God, ****. I know it's hard, I know it hurts so bad, but put on some gospel music and just thank Him. Thank Him and praise Him like you never had before. Cast your burdens on Him and just cry to Him. Let it all out and He'll be there for you, He'll comfort you, He'll answer your prayers and give you encouragement. Just listen to Him, remember to thank Him and praise Him every day, praise Him for allowing you to be with **** and ****, praise Him for making a way for **** and **** to be un- separated, praise Him that dad is fighting for you, praise Him that you can speak to Him, praise Him for being there, praise Him for not leaving you, praise Him for your health, praise Him that you can contact us, praise Him that **** is okay, praise Him that dad is in good health, praise Him that you and the rest of your family is in good health, but most of all, praise Him because He will answer our prayers. He will answer your prayers, ****. He will never leave us or forsake us, and He has already answered our prayers. Just open up that Bible and claim those scriptures, and never ever forget to praise Him and thank Him. Thank Him for this experience, because when you come out of this battlefield and you stomp on that Devil one more time, you can walk with your head held high and know that God brought you through, Mom, Me, and Dad. Baby girl, don't cry, okay? Keep your head up because we have the victory. I am always here for you, ****Oh baby girl, I know it's hard, honey. I know it's hard and it hurts me so much to know that you're hurting like this. Just remember to call on Jesus. He'll answer, ****. He knows the plan He has for us, baby sister, and He'll never forsake us. Praise God with all your heart and all your soul and stomp on that Devil, **** we have the victory, remember that. And you make sure that **** reads this because this is for her, too. I love you, **** I know that you take things to the heart, and that's a gift God has given you, believe it or not. You are a prayer warrior. You are so strong-minded and outspoken. You are strong, baby girl. You are SOO strong. Keep your head up, little sister, keep it up for me. Both of you stay strong. You guys aren't in this alone. We are here for you, we are behind you, and we are fighting for you. **** and ****. Encourage each other in the Lord and He will give you everything you need to sustain yourselves and see this thing through, because the Lord has a purpose for our family. Thank God and praise Him, young ones. I don't want to leave, but I'm going to let dad write you guys, too. We love you guys so much and we are praying for you and the rest of our family. Keep in touch with the boys and ****, too. We love you so much. Keep your head up and smile, okay? I love you guys. Here's dad.

All of my love,

Brother **** sent us this and dad wants me to give it to you guys:

CHILDREN'S PRAYER
ANDREWS FAMILY

And God upholds all things by the word of His power

1. You are the head and not the tail, above only and not beneath. (Deuteronomy 28;13)
2. No weapon formed against you shall prosper. isaiah 54;17
3. God has not given you a spirit of fear but of power, love and a sound mind (2 Timothy 1;7)
4. You have the mind of Christ and you can do all things through Christ who strengthens you. (1st Corinthians 2;16;Philippians 4;13)
5. You are Jesus' little sheep and the voice of a stranger, you will not follow (John 10;3-5)
6. You obey your parents and you will enjoy long life (Ephesians 6.2)
7. You have a circumcised heart and you love The Lord your God with all your heart and soul (Deuteronomy 30;6)
8. You have hidden God's Word in your heart so that you will not sin against him (Psalm 119; 11)
9. Gods Word is a lamp unto your feet and a light to your path. You're surrounded with favor like a shield (Psalm 119;105; 5;12)
10. You have the joy of the Lord as your strength Nehemiah 8;10

Praise the lord sweetheart. The lord is our strength and he will never let us down. We often shed tears but victory is always ours. The sun is shining in spite of the clouds. This is the attitude we must take. No man rules our life except Jesus Christ. He looks like he is far away at times but we always see another day and another sun. The tears are hard to take. But remember your family will always be there. Your dad has not forgotten his children. I have another lawyer in Colorado and another here. Continue to be faithful to the lord Jesus Christ. Never let yourself become depressed. Encourage your brothers and sisters. Continue to write your letters and express your desires. Do this every chance you get. Always remember my phone numbers. Call collect whenever you can. Pray in English and in tongues every day and every night. When you write, remember it is important to write your mind. Thanks for the great letter tonight. My love for you children is great. You are a great inspiration to multitudes. I love you. You will be returned home to me. Yesterday is gone. Because we ask him to, he has forgiven our sins. Today we have a new task. Live to please him and watch him bring us joy in the midst of all our problems. I love you. I am not there but I am praying daily day and night for my sweethearts **** and ****, **** and ****. Keep your faith, hope, smiles, and joy. You are the children of a king, (Jesus Christ). You are my sons and daughters filled with the love beyond measure and the ability to be the best in all that you think or do. You have the Holy Ghost. Wipe away your tears and smile. I love you. ****, ****, ****, and ****.

Your dad.

**** Wrote:

I am still upset at the family and is it wrong to not claim them because I don't feel that they should even call themselves loyal to this family. They don't deserve my love. But anyways when are you graduating be sure to take lots and lots of pictures 4 me ok? Because I am going to put them up in my room. So when are you and dad going to come out here because we all miss you. You should see **** he is about to get his teeth and he can say nice its so adorable and he's getting ready to walk. Me and **** practice with him everyday. He can take a few steps but other then that he's doing good. Yeah when you talk to **** tell him that we all love him ok? And congratulations on graduating. I am really proud of you but I will let you go now.

Tell brother **** thank you for the wonderful scriptures and I love you ****.

Love always your baby sister ****

Hi Dad

How are you doing so if I race you around the block who will win me of course but thanks dad for the lovely letter I really needed it so I will not give up on God. I am trying to pray in tongues again but I need more faith in God I really miss you and **** I really would like to see you guys soon do you know if they changed the date yet because I really don't want to give up on my family. Dad if you only knew what we are going through it would break your heart. It has already broken my heart. Dad I love you so much. I have faith that you will get us back it's hard being away from you and **** because I never would of thought that something like this would happen to our family. I know that everything happens for a reason and I know that God never gives us anything that we can't handle; but I am still upset at the family because they could at least, Have tried to get us. Instead they lied but it's ok because I have God on my side. Well dad I will let you go now. **** Said to tell you that she loves you and keep us in your prayers. Well dad I love you and I thank you for being my Dad and my friend. I love you so much dad. well I'll let you go now.

Love your one and only little sugarplum

**** Wrote:

Hey baby girls ...I'm sorry we missed you guys yesterday, but everything happens for a purpose. Y'all missed out on some paper tho! lol But I gave **** that CD of those songs we were telling you guys about so she could give it to you guys. I burned one for you guys, the boys, and **** and I hope they play because I've burned a few CDs on my laptop and they didn't play very well. If they don't work then you guys have the artist's name (Martha Munizzi I think her name is) and the title of the album (The Best Is Yet To Come), so you guys can find it somewhere. I'm glad to hear you guys are encouraged. I don't want you guys to ever give up or feel down, because no one and nothing can separate us from the heart without our permission, so you guys remember that and be defiant. That's wonderful that **** is close to walking now. He's so precious. Why did **** say you can't talk to ****? We'll talk to them about that for you guys. I don't see what the problem is. He's not involved in the case at all. That's ridiculous and we'll be here giving them a piece of our minds about that. It's bad enough that you guys haven't talked to him or seen him in over a year, that's just sick that they're trying to delay you guys' being in contact even more. They disgust me. I'll tell dad and we're gonna talk to them about that. That's not okay. Speaking of ****, we were trying to get them to let him come with us to see you guys but they said no. I have to discuss that further with them. I was going to yesterday, but the man who takes care of all that was in a meeting. I'm planning on going up there after graduation to see you all, so I'm going to try to make arrangements so we can all see each other, us kids, ****, and dad and maybe mom too, if she's out. I was thinking of maybe taking **** and the boys along****actually as soon as I'm finished writing this, so that's in effect and I'll write you guys regarding it. Oh and thank you for the congratulations. I'm SOOOOO excited!!! :-D I just turned the calendar to June today and I realized that I only have like hardly even TWO weeks!!! :-D All I have to do is keep up with my homework!!! :-D lol speaking of homework, that's why I stayed home from school today. I got on my email to check school loop, which is a program where we get our homework sent to us in the mail, and after I got my homework I decided to write you guys back cause I hate to leave your emails in the box without opening them and replying. Yeah I missed a few assignments when I was gone. Yes, they gave us the new court date. I think. I think dad said he got it. If he didn't, then he'll reply and let you guys know. I'll tell brother**** you guys said thank you. And ****, remember these letters are for both of you guys, so you read them, too and hit me back. I'm glad you are inspired and I don't want you guys to give up. Just hold on to God and He'll direct our paths. Just stay close to Him and He'll guide you every day. He will give you peace because He promised that to the saints. He knows what He's doing. Keep your faith. I love you guys. I'm gonna get started on my homework. Dad isn't here yet, but when he does come, he'll write you guys back, too. Love you baby sisters. Keep your heads up always and keep your eyes looking forwards.

All my love,

Praise the lord sweetheart. You are still my number one baby girl Sugar Plum. Remember DAVID. He was the son of a bondwoman or slave. He was just a shepherd among his seven brothers and his dad. Yet God chose him to be king. You have been chosen to be one of God's anointed and nothing can take that away from you. Never allow yourself to feel depressed or discouraged. God sees every tear and according to his bible, he puts them in a bottle before him.

The sorrow that you feel is greater in my heart than in yours and that of your brothers and sisters. **** I came to see you children on the 30 of May but we could not see you girls. We saw the boys. I do have a complaint to my lawyer. You have suffered a lot and many lies have been written on you children and myself according to the reports that I have received. Yet remember that yesterday is gone and our sins forgiven if we ask the lord Jesus to forgive us. So forget about yesterday. Do as David did. He was discouraged and fallen but God raised him up again and he was so rich he gave over 89 million in gold and silver to the lord's work. His son was the wisest in the world. He is the only man that God says is a king forever right now in heaven outside of Jesus Christ. God gave you children a promise. It has to happen. You four will be a part of this last day work of God. The things you are going through will help prepare you to stand on God's truth and not take down. I love your stand for right. You are forgiven for your wrong. I love you. Be faithful and steadfast. Do not move from right. Be encouraged. I am working night and day with two lawyers and two lawsuits. Talk to the boys as often as you can. Pray in tongues and remember that your spirit knows a lot better than you and I what to pray for. Pray also in English daily. As you pray thank God for answering the desires of you heart. He lives in the midst of your praises and thanks. In your greatest sorrows learn to praise and thank him the most. The Joy of The Lord is your strength. Never lose your joy. I love you and give my love to all the family every time you see them. Your dad is always by your side. Remember that there is only one**** Sugar Plum. I will still win the race around the block. You children have shown marvelous strength in going through those things without your parents standing by your side. You have shown the spirit that brings success in spite of all opposition. Set you goals and none can stop you from achieving them. Dad

**** Wrote:

Hey **** thanks for the letter I was really upset that I didn't get to see you or dad but I'm not mad but anyways I was mad that **** said that we couldn't talk to **** she never told me why though and little **** is walking now and he says nice, thank you, please and I LOVE YOU. I taught him how to say I love you and thank you. Our foster parent taught him how to say nice and I am working on getting him how to say please. He is really good at talking though and he screams a lot. Still I can't wait until you guys come out here again. Anyways, thanks for the CDS we didn't get them yet but we will. I so proud of my sister she's graduating awwwww how cute my sisters all grown up. Well she thinks she's all grown up. But anyways we are stronger than ever with you and dads words. They really do encourage us to be motivated and never to give up. So thank you for being there for us all the way. So does dad know when the next court date is so I can be there and do you know what jail mom is in? She is in jail isn't she? Can you give me you and dad's #s again? They tell us that we're not allowed to have them but I don't care what they say and when you and dad come out here can you bring me a copy of the books that dad wrote please? And keep praying for us because I do believe that God will bring us out of this fight. I am trying to think about the good things because the good things are what's keeping my head up so how is**** and you doing? Good hopefully. Are you guys still getting married? So how's dad doing? I am still going to write him. I can't believe that your going to be 18. That's crazy! Look at all the time we lost on our family time. We barely even know each other. That's crazy. Don't you think? Well like you said, everything happens for a reason. I still believe in you and dad so don't let me down now. Here's**** I love you **** here's ****

Hi**** how is everything out there? How's dad doing? Is he in good health? I hope so. So have you heard from mom? How is she doing? Thank you for the letter and I believe that dad will get us back. I just don't want to leave**** here by himself because I know that they wont give him to dad and nobody in our family is trying to get him. That's the only thing holding me back but I do want to go with dad. But you know how the system is. Anyways how's the family doing? Good? Hopefully? How's princess doing? I saw her in the pictures that you sent. **** You guys were just looking 2 bomb but anyways **** told me that your graduating. CONGRADULATIONS!!!!!!!!!! Who would of thought of you graduating? That's good! I am proud of you. I just can't wait until I graduate now, but I can't wait to see you and dad when you come out here, I don't know if they will let you see **** though because mom doesn't have custody of him anymore, but we'll see. Well I will let you go now because **** wants to talk or write to dad now. I love you ****.

Hi Dad how have you been doing lately? I can't wait to see you when you come out here. **** Is excited too. So how is everything going out there? How is the family and the church doing? Hopefully everything and everybody is doing good. I can't wait until we move back with you. I don't know if **** wants to go back because she doesn't want to leave **** here alone because I don't think that you can get him. But I am praying and keeping the faith in God so I know everything happens for a reason and I know that he has a plan for me and my family. I have been stressing a lot lately because the court date is so close. But I will make it through. So dad you still think that you can beat me around the block? Just wait until I get out there. We'll see who will win. Well dad, thank you for that encouraging letter that you wrote. It really encourages me to keep on going and not to give up on God. I am finding myself praying a lot more lately. I really do believe that you can get us back and God will help you dad. I love you so much please get us back. I don't want to live my life like this anymore. I am tired of being away from my loved ones. It's getting harder every day and I don't know how long I can take it. I really want to run away and take a greyhound out there but I am patiently waiting until the court date. Well dad please continue to pray and write me. Thank you dad for everything your doing to get us back. I love you so much dad and always remember that you are my best friend and I love you for that always. Well here's **** Love ****

Hi Dad how are you doing? How is everybody out there doing? Good I hope. Well I was thinking about the court date and I am a little nervous. I still have faith in my family and I still believe that God will bring us out of this battle. But I don't want to leave **** because he's still a baby and I know that the county wont let you adopt him that's the only thing that's holding me back from going

**** has already made up her mind she wants to go with you and she wants the**** to go to but I don't think they will let you have him but I am still praying to God that he will touch their hearts and let us go because they don't tell us everything that is going on with our case so we kind of have to force them to tell us even though they don't tell us the whole truth. We learn later what the truth is. Well dad thank you for the letter. It really took a burden off of me. Well dad I will let you go now so I love you and keep praying for us. Where there is a will there is a way. God Bless dad. I love you. Love always. Your daughter ****

**** Wrote:

Hey my little honeys!!!
What up Lil miss? How are you doing? Yeah I know what you mean. I was upset too when we couldn't see you guys. How come you guys didn't come? Oh here's our numbers:

home
dad's cell
church

Awwww I'm missing my sweet little ****. That's how you spell his name? He's a Lil angel! I miss you all so much. lol that's funny that he screams a lot cause so does ****' son ****. He's my Lil angel, too. Yeah I told you guys I was planning on going out there this summer after I graduate, right? Thanks for the Congratulations!!! ☺ Oh my goodness, girl tomorrow's my last real day in high school!!!! I'm so excited. Yeah we are growing up fast. It sucks how this is the only year we would all be in high school that we missed out. But that's okay cause there's still COLLEGE!!!!!!! ☺ ☺☺ It's gonna be SOOOOO fun!!!! Yeah and make sure you get that CD from **** cause it's wonderful. And if you don't get it, then at least you know what it's called n stuff. I'm very happy to hear that you guys are feeling better about this situation. I know how important it is to be encouraged, especially when times are so hard like they are now. We're not giving up on you guys, so you guys don't give up on us cause it's gonna be okay. No I don't know what jail mom is in I would guess that she's in county, but I don't know if she's still there now. Yeah I'll try to remember to bring you guys the books. After I finish writing back, I'm gonna study for my finals tomorrow and so I may or may not put the books aside tonight so I'll write that down. **** And I are I dunno. He's just different. Maybe we'll get back together, maybe not. I'm really getting fed up with him being so irresponsible and childish. But I do love him and I do want to work things out. He's just not meeting me half way. Oh well, that's up to God in the end. Dad's doing really well. I've been stressing out a lot lately. Why? I dunno, I just have. I think everything that I've been holding down is now starting to surface and I just am feeling the pain everywhere I go. Nah, hon, don't say we barely know each other. We're blood, sis, and we don't know each other only if we choose not to. Yeah, we're not next to each other all the time, but that's just a circumstance. It's nothing to keep us from being close. Like I said before, no one can change us but us. We are as close as we allow ourselves to be. No one dictates what we share with each other, how we respond to each other, etc. but us. Therefore, no one tells us how close we are but us because what we want we will get. All we have to do is take that step. The only hard thing is making sure we take the right step. I love you too, Chickita. So what are you going to be doing this summer? I want to get another job and save for college. I need to pray more and meditate on the word more. I am so stressed out and I need God's guidance right now so bad. Everything will work out the way it's supposed to. Dad told you the court date, right? You guys are going to be there for sure, right? I hope so. Have you guys talked to the boys? You have **** email address, right? Yeah we are going to talk to them about ****. He's going to turn himself in I guess on Friday, tomorrow, and from there, I'm hoping they transfer his probation to California so he can get out of that hellhole. Well Chickita, I'm going to write **** because I'm exhausted and I still have studying to do. I love you baby girl. Chin up, eyes forward, face of flint. Be defiant but wise always. I love you baby sister.

Love always,
a.k.a. the Queen

p.s.

Oh yeah **** is doing well and she says Hi and she loves you guys. What's the deal chick? You sure haven't written me in a while! It's good to hear from you. Thank you for the congratulations. I wish so much you guys could be there. I would hecca kick everyone off the guest list except for us kids n dad n **** lol. Dad is in wonderful health and we are doing as well as we can be without you guys here to share the days with. Well one of the many good things we can appreciate out of this experience is the appreciation that I have now for every tiny little detail of what it is to be a family. You hear so many people saying it, and we know very well now, etched in our souls, how important we are to each other. I hope you are being encouraged, sweet sister. We all need it, and now that we are feeling the burden more, we need to encourage each other so much. Every single one of us, from us girls to the boys to dad, all of us need to know and understand, remember and never let leave our minds the fact that we are family and we are strong and we will be together again. Don't worry kid, we're going to get ****, too. He is our blood, too and we're not going to leave him behind for nothing. Don't be afraid because we all know in the bottom of our hearts what is right and what is fair, and God is on our side, so don't you worry about a thing, ****. Don't rush to graduate, though. It is a great feeling, but ...well let me just explain it like this: All year I've been counting down days on the school calendar, waiting for weeks sometimes just so I could cross out a bunch of days all at once. Then this last Monday came around. And I don't even want to take the thing out of my binder to look at it, much less cross off any more days. I am FREAKING OUT!!!! lol Oh my GOODNESS I'm so excited!!! Man I wish you guys could be here. But it's all gravy, like I told ****, we still have college. You guys will be there in my heart, every single one of you kids and mom and ****. I'm SO taking a billion pictures and videotaping it!!! loll Well I'm gonna go and start on my studies so I don't freak out too much tomorrow. I love you little sister. Keep praying, you and **** both, and never give up. Like I told ****, Chin up, eyes forward, face of flint. Be defiant but wise always. I love you baby girl.

Love always,
****. A.k.a. the Queen ☺

here's dad
Praise The Lord sweetheart. The joy of the lord is our strength. I AM GLAD TO SEE THE LORD HAS PUT SOME MORE JOY BACK INTO YOUR HEARTS. The court date is supposed to be July 12 is what **** told us. My lawyer has not given me the date yet. She is moving the court from the county to a different county. Continue to pray daily. When we began to pray and get on one accord, God begins to move. **** Was worried about ****. You can't help ****by saying you want to stay there for him. Your reason does not matter. The court will only hear that you want to stay. You defeat the purpose of our court battle if you want to stay for any reason. The question the court want to know is do you or don't you want to go home now. The reports written by **** and told to the court by their lawyer say you girls don't want to go home. We have included ***** in our civil rights case. You five children have a claim to **** because he is considered your sibling. You can only bring him to where you are. Where will you bring him to if you are in Colorado? If **** stayed she would only be a babysitter for **** for his adopted family. She could not help him or herself. Keep praying. I am seeing a man in the morning that is going to be very helpful at the coming court date. Expect to be home soon. There

is a reason for you being there so far. I believe that that time is over. Be encouraged and pray daily. Pray both in tongue and in English. God has now begun to move. Let them know at every chance that you want to come home. **** Will be here also. He may not get here until after the civil law suit but he will be here. Stay holy, stay honest and godly. Encourage the boys. Always make it known that you all want to come home. Several TV networks have heard about you children. One may come out to talk to you all. Let them know that you want to come home if they talk to you children. I love you. Stay strong. Be not afraid of the lies. You will be home soon. By you being strong you bring strength to so many others. I love you. The Lord will never allow you to be ashamed. Dad

**** Wrote: Hi **** how are things going? Yes I have **** e-mail I've been writing him but he hasn't written me back but that's ok. Anyways, yes were going to be there at the court date. I can't wait to see you and dad. I feel so bad that we can't be there at your graduation. I'm sorry **** because I really wanted to be there for you but anyways don't even stress about the situation because God has a plan for each and everyone of us so don't even trip off what they say because they don't know what God has in store for us. Where is **** at? Is he out there? I really hope that they let us see him because I really miss him. Have you talked to mom yet? Nobody has heard from her. I really hope that she goes to the court date. I don't want to get my hopes up too high about going home because I know God doesn't make things happen but he allows them to happen and I just hope God lets us go back. **** Said Hi!!!!! But yeah how was your last real day of High School? Was it emotional because I know it would be emotional for me. I would be crying. Were you sad or happy? Well I am really nervous and scared about the court date me and **** are counting down. We have 28 days until the court date. So have they told you which county we will be at because they haven't told us anything yet. All the information we're getting is from you and dad. Well I don't know. I really hope that they give us to dad and that they give **** to him too because there still talking about the adoption. Everybody is keeping the whole adoption thing away from us. So I don't know what's going on with that but yeah so how is dad? Is he doing good? We haven't talked to the boys in a while. They are always busy and now that it's summer, I know for a fact that they are going to be really busy. Well we are not going on our vacation anymore. I don't know why so I guess we are just going to be getting summer jobs and going to Eliges. You know 6 flags Eliges gardens. Yeah nothing much though but anyways sorry I didn't write back sooner. I haven't been on the computer in a long time. Anyways I try to keep my mind clear off the whole situation because it's just so stressing. If the county takes mom and dads parental rights I don't know what I will do. Gosh they'll have to lock me up for murder. No I am just playing but it would be too hard. I will probably have a break down. It will be so hard having to start over with these people. My heart will be torn to pieces but I am still trying to keep the faith and strength to get through this. It is only a matter of time before all this is over and done with. Man, I miss you and dad so much and we didn't come because they didn't tell us that you guys were here. They told us when you guys were already on the road because this is what happened. We were going to go to our homeboy's graduation but we ended up not going. Then like 1 "o" clock. **** Our foster mom comes in and says, "ow your dad was here and he wanted to see you guys but I told them that you guys were going to go to a graduation. Did you guys want to see him?" Then **** said, "No I'm fine he's gone anyways." Then I said, "well I wanted to see him.

I wouldn't have gone to the graduation if I had known that my dad was coming. Can't he just turn around?" Then **** said, "Well I'm sorry. I just thought that you guys wanted to go to the graduation so I told them no. Your not mad are you?" Then **** said no and I said well it doesn't matter now if he's gone. Yeah I was pretty upset but that's why we didn't get to call you that day either. Because my therapist said that you were on the road. She was upset at **** too because she was down there waiting for us. But what's in the past is in the past. So there's nothing I can do. So anyways **** has an e-mail address it is**** you can write her if you want. But yeah, anyways and don't forget to bring the books, ok? Well I love you and I'll let you go now. Always the baby of the girls. **** Your baby sister I love you ****.

Hi Dad how are you doing this fine evening? I was really glad to hear from you. Every time you write, it always encourages and motivates me to be my best at everything. I do thank you dad for the letter. I have been praying night and day for God to bring us out of this battle and he is going to do it. Have they switched the county yet? Because I have been waiting for an answer. So dad how is the church doing? I hope they're keeping us in their prayers. I am a little nervous and scared at the same time and anxious to find out what God has in store for us on the 12th of July. Me and **** have been counting down. I am afraid of what they will do. I don't want to be separated from my family any longer then I have to. I am staying strong only because I know that God has a plan for this family and I do believe that he will touch their hearts and let us go back with you. I am happy that God has put Joy back into my heart. Also it has been a tough battle and I am ready for it to end. I am scared of what the results will be though because it can go both ways. We can go back home with you or we can still be separated.

I am praying to God that he lets us go back with you. I am proud of you Dad and thankful to have you as my dad because YOU NEVER GAVE UP ON US. When everybody else did you didn't. You stayed in my heart because I knew that you wouldn't give up on us until the end. Even now that it is the end you are still here waiting for us to come home. You are still here fighting for us and I love you so much for that. God has really blessed our family. He has blessed us with you. To me you are my ANGEL dad and I thank you for not giving up on us. On your kids. On me. Thank you so much. Now I know that everything happens for a reason. I love you so much dad. Thank you for all you done and all your doing still till this day. Well dad I think I will let you go now. Thank you dad for everything you are doing. I have never seen anyone as strong as you are. I love you dad, love always. Your little sugar plum also known as your little sweetheart **** I LOVE YOU DAD!!!!!!!!!!!

P.S Thanks dad for everything you've ever done for us.

**** Wrote:

Hey **** I'm not going to all the way reply right now. I just wanted to tell you that you guys are gonna be called on to testify in court to tell them that you want to come home. I'm going to finish writing you later I just wanted to make sure that you got this. Love you baby sister.

****Thanks ****4 the update I understand I love you so much

AMERICA'S SECRET CHILDREN'S PRISON'S

FOSTER. ADOPTION, TRANSITIONAL
WHERE ???? HOW ???? WHY????

1. **MY COMPLAINT**

MY LETTER MAY SEEM INSIGNIFICANT WHEN I CONSIDER THE GREAT RESPONSIBILITY OF YOUR POSITION. YET I WRITE TODAY OF A PRACTICE THAT I CONSIDER A GREATER THREAT TO AMERICA THAN ANY FOREIGN POWER. THE ABILITY OF THE HUMAN RESOURCE AGENCIES, THE CHILD PROTECTIVE AGENCIES, FAMILY COURTS, WELFARE CONNECTED AGENCIES, AND VARIOUS OTHER CHILD CONNECTED GROUPS TO REMOVE A CHILD FROM A HOME OR TO WITHOLD A CHILD FROM A PARENT WITHOUT A PARENT'S PROVEN GUILT.

ONCE THE CHILD IS REMOVED FROM THE HOME, THE CHILD IS CONSIDERED A WARD OF THE COURT OR THE STATE. THE CHILDREN ARE OFTEN HELD IN LOCKED FACILITIES WITH EITHER NO CONTACT OR LIMITED CONTACT WITH THEIR FAMILIES OR PARENTS. BASIC PRISON RULES ARE INSTITUTED WITH ANY VISITS SUPERVISED AND CONVERSATIONS MONITERED BY THE PRESENCE OF AN ASSIGNED PERSON WITHIN HEARING

RANGE OR THROUGH GLASS WINDOWS OR TWO WAY MIRRORS. ANY CHILD THAT REFUSES TO CO-OPORATE IS DISCIPLINED ACCORDINGLY ALONG MODIFIED PRISON RULES.

RUNAWAYS ARE TREATED AS FUGITIVES FROM JUSTICE. A PERSON THAT HELPS A RUNAWAY TO RETURN HOME IS CONSIDERED HELPING AN ESCAPEE AND IS TREATED THE SAME AS IF THE CHILD ESCAPED FROM A PRISON. ANY PARENT OR FAMILY MEMBER THAT SEEKS TO RETRIEVE A CHILD PER THEIR MATERNAL OR GOD GIVEN PROTECTIVE SPIRIT IS CONSIDERED A KIDNAPER AND FACES FELONY CHARGES.

STATEWIDE OR NATIONWIDE ALERTS CAN BE PUT OUT ON THE CHILD AND FAMILY MEMBER PUTTING THEM BOTH IN DANGER OF PHYSICAL VIOLENCE OR POSSIBLE DEATH WHEN CONFRONTED BY LAW ENFORCEMENT OFFICIALS. THESE CONFRONTATIONS ARE INCREASING BUT UNFORTUNATELY ONLY THE FAMILY MEMBERS ARE CONSIDERED CRIMINALS. BY VIRTUE OF THEIR OCCUPATION, THE AGENCY PERSONNEL ARE ALWAYS RIGHT EXCEPT IN THE USE OF EXCESSIVE FORCE AT THE TIME OF THE REMOVAL.

IN ONE YEAR ALONE OVER THREE HUNDRED FIFTY THOUSAND (350,000) FAMILY ABDUCTIONS OCCURRED. I WILL ASK THE QUESTION MANY TIMES IN THIS WRITING WHY SHOULD OVER THREE HUNDRED THOUSAND PARENTS FEEL IT NECESSARY TO RISK PRISON AND EVEN DEATH TO KIDNAP THEIR OWN CHILDREN?

MOST AMERICANS ARE NOT AWARE OF THE SCOPE OF THE PROBLEM. WHY? BECAUSE THIS IS A PRIVATE AND EMBARRISING PROBLEM? WHO WANTS THE WORLD TO KNOW THAT I HAVE LOST MY CHILDREN? THEY WILL ALL THINK THAT I AM AN UNFIT PARENT.

OUT OF HOME PLACEMENT IS A MORE DIGNIFIED WAY TO SAY <u>A CHILD IS A PRISONER AND THE PARENTS ARE ON PAROLE OR A FAMILY IS BEING RULED AND CONTROLED BY THE STATE</u>. BOTH THE CHILD AND THE PARENT CAN BE TOTALLY IGNORED OR SILENCED FROM SPEAKING BY THE AGENCY IN VOLATION OF BOTH THE HUMAN RESOURCE CODE AND THE CIVIL RIGHTS CODE.

<u>THE ABILITY TO USE ALLEGATIONS ONLY TO DENY EITHER A PARENT OR A CHILD THEIR INDIVIDUAL OR FAMILY CIVIL RIGHTS, PLACES AMERICA IN A LEGAL DICTATORSHIP ROLE FROM THESE CHILDREN CONNECTED AGENCIES AND OFFICES. THESE AGENCIES AND OFFICES ARE ESTABLISHED AND GUIDED BY FEDERAL GUIDELINES. THE BUCK STOPS AT THE TOP. A DOG IS MOVED BY IT'S HEAD; NOT IT'S TAIL. ACCOUNTABILITY SHOULD NOT BE GIVEN TO A COUNTY, STATE, OR INDIVIDUAL WITHOUT CONSCIENTIOUS OVERSIGHT. TO DELEGATE DICTATORSHIP CHALLENGES OUR FREEDOM.</u>

THE MOST ARROGANT AND INDEPENDENT FAMILY CONTROL SYSTEM IN AMERICA HAS PROVEN ITSELF TO BE THE FAMILY COURT SYSTEM CONNECTED WITH THE

U.S. DEPARTMENT OF HEALTH AND HUMAN SERVICES ADMINISTRATION FOR CHILDREN AND FAMILIES. IT IS OPEN KNOWLEDGE THROUGHOUT THE COURT SYSTEM THAT THIS SECTION OF THE SYSTEM HAS BEEN LABLED UNTOUCHABLE AND A PRIVATE DICTATOR BY OTHER COURT SYSTEMS.

TO FALSELY LABEL A PARENT GUILTY OF SEXUAL ABUSE, PHYSICAL ABUSE OR MENTAL ABUSE OF EITHER A CHILD OR A SPOUSE FOR THE SAKE OF GAINING FEDERAL FUNDS OR TO PROTECT AN ADOPTION OPERATION SHOULD BE A CRIMINAL OFFENSE. TO SEEK TO JUSTIFY ANY ILLEGAL OR UNWARRANTED ACTION AGAINST A CHILD, PARENT OR THEIR FAMILY SHOULD BE A CRIMINAL OFFENSE. ACCORDING TO AMERICA'S JUSTICE SYSTEM, THIS IS A CRIMINAL OFFENSE.

TO REFUSE TO SEEK TO REUNITE A FAMILY AND INSTEAD TO FARM A CHILD OUT TO A FOSTER PARENT OR SEND A CHILD TO A WAITING ADOPTION HOME UNDER THE GUISE OF UNFIT PARENT, UNSAFE HOME, UNABLE TO PROVIDE, TOO OLD, CANNOT CONTROL THE CHILD OR ANY OTHER CONCOTED REASON, SHOULD BE A CRIMINAL OFFENSE. ACCORDING TO OUR AMERICAN JUSTICE SYSTEM, THIS IS A CRIMINAL OFFENSE.

WHAT HAPPENS WHEN A COURT SYSTEM OR THE ENFORCEMENT ARM OF OUR GOVERNMENT SANCTIONS THIS TYPE OF ACTIVITY? THE COURT SYSTEM OR THE ENFORCEMENT ARM BECOMES THE DICTATOR BUT THE GOVERNMENT MUST SANCTION THEIR ACTIVITY.

THIS I CALL POCKET DICTATORSHIP OR DELEGATED DICTATORSHIP. THE GOVERNMENT IS RESPONSIBLE FOR THE ACTION OF ITS BRANCHES. POCKET DICTATORSHIP HAS BECOME A COMMON PRACTICE IN OUR AMERICAN JUSTICE SYSTEM AND MOST AMERICANS HAVE ACCEPTED THIS WITHOUT QUESTION.

ONE LAWMAKER STATED TO ME THAT THE CHILDREN'S COURT IS UNTOUCHABLE. THEIR DECISIONS ARE ALWAYS FINAL IN HIS EYES. MAYBE THIS LAWMAKER IS NOT AWARE THAT ALL CRIMINALS OR LAWBREAKERS ARE NOT IN THE STREETS OR SERVING IN OTHER COURTS. SOME WEAR WHITE COLLARS, SOME WEAR ROBES AND SOME ARE IN LAW ENFORCEMENT POSITIONS, BOTH ON THE STREETS AND IN THE COURTS. THIS SAME LAWMAKER WAS ABLE TO SPEAK THE OUTCOME OF MANY CASES BEFORE THEY WERE HEARD BY OBSERVING WHICH JUDGE OR MAGISTRATE THE CASE WOULD COME BEFORE. WHAT HE WAS REALLY SAYING WAS THAT I HAVE CLOSED MY EYES AND EARS TO ONE BRANCH OF OUR SYSTEM. THE REST STILL MERITS MY ATENTION. HE HAD GIVEN UP HIS FREEDOM IN THIS AREA. HE IS A SLAVE. HE SITS AS A WILLFULLY BLIND JUDGE IN THE MATTERS THAT HE CHOSE TO BE BLIND IN. FAMILY LAW INVOLVING CHILDREN IS THE MOST CRITICAL ARM OF OUR JUSTICE SYSTEM BECAUSE IT CAN DIRECT AND SHAPE A PATH FOR THE REST OF A PERSON'S LIFE.

2. <u>YOUR CHILD WILL NOT RETURN</u>

NOBLE NAMES DOES NOT ALWAYS MEAN NOBLE CAUSES. A CHILDREN'S CRUSADE TO WIN BACK THE HOLY LAND MAY HAVE SOUNDED LIKE A GREAT IDEA IN MEDEVIAL DAYS TO SOME THAT PROMOTED THE CRUSADES AS A GESTURE OF FAITH. WAS IT REALLY A GESTURE OF FAITH OR A SUICIDE MISSION FOR A GROUP OF MISLED CHILDREN BEING MANIPULATED FOR THAT DAY'S POLITICAL GAIN? I AGREE WITH HISTORY. IT WAS A SUICIDE MISSION WITH A HIDDEN AGENDA. MEDEVIAL NEWS PROPAGANDA WAS CALLED OUT. RELIGIOUS ZEALOTS WERE RECRUITED. URGENCY OF THE MOMENT WAS PROMOTED. INNOCENT CHILDREN WERE THE PAWNS IN A GAME OF DEATH.

MOST COUNTRIES TODAY HAVE ENOUGH CARE AND RESPECT FOR CHILDREN NOT TO SEND THEM AROUND THE WORLD ON A MILITARY CRUSADE TO RECLAIM A COUNTRY OR CITY WHEN IT IS IN THE HANDS OF BARBARIANS WHO HOLD NO REGARD FOR THE LIFE OF CHILDREN. ESPECIALLY CHILDREN THAT ARE EXPECTED TO DESTROY THE BARBARIAN PLAYGROUND. HOWEVER, OUR OWN COUNTRY OF AMERICA HAS ALLOWED OUR CHILDREN TO BE PLACED IN A PICK AND CHOOSE POOL FOR ADOPTION AND OUT OF HOME REMOVAL WHILE TYING THE HANDS OF THEIR PARENTS. REGARDLESS OF

WHAT THE LAW SAYS, YOUR CHILD IS NOT PROGRAMED TO RETURN HOME IN MANY INSTANCES.

THIS IS NOT A PROGRAM FOR THE RICH. IN OVER THIRTY YEARS OF WORKING WITH THOSE IN OUT OF HOME PLACEMENT AND ADOPTION CANDIDATES, I HAVE NOT FOUND ONE RICH CHILD. HOW DID THIS HAPPEN? HOW CAN A COUNTY PUBLISH AND ADVERTISE A LIST OF PARENT'S CHILDREN THAT THEY WANT TO ADOPT OUT IN THE FACE OF THE PARENTS THAT ARE QUALIFIED AND INNOCENT OF ANY OF THE CHARGES THAT THEY ARE ACCUSED OF?

IN MANY INSTANCES, THE FAILURE TO PROTECT A CHILD WHILE IN THE CUSTODY OF CHILD RELATED AGENCIES IS GROSSLY WORSE THAN THE REASON THE CHILD WAS REMOVED. A PERSON CAN WAIT ONE YEAR AND RECEIVE YOUR CHILD FROM A GIVEAWAY FEDERALLY BACKED AMERICAN SYSTEM WHILE A PARENT MUST STAND BACK WATCHING AND OBSERVING. HIS LIPS ARE SEALED AND HIS HANDS TIED OFFICIALLY BY A COURT. IS IT TIME FOR AMERICANS TO DEMAND A CHANGE OR REVERT TO THIS OFFICIAL**** LEGAL SLAVE TRADE *** APPROVED BY YOUR LEGISLATURE SEE SLAV@. FR/ SLAVE.*

I COULD IMAGINE A PRESENT DAY AD DESCRIPTION SAYING *****TERRA, A SEVEN YEAR OLD BOY FOR ADOPTION. WELL MANNERED WITH C AVERAGE IN SCHOOL. HIS MOTHER IS A COOK AND UNKNOWN FATHER. **** MAYBE ONE SAYING FRANCES A FOURTEEN

YEAR OLD. LAST REPORT CARD HAD ONE A, TWO C'S AND TWO D'S. LIKES TO BAKE CAKES. RE MOVED FROM HER HOME BECAUSE NEIGHBOR SAID SHE WAS ON HER PORCH WITH OTHER TEENS AFTER CURFEW. OR WHAT ABOUT THE MAN THAT PHYSICALY PUT HIS CHILD IN HIS SUV WHEN HIS FIVE YEAR OLD WANTED TO STAY AND PLAY WITH HER FRIENDS AT SCHOOL. THE AD. WOULD POSSIBLY SAY. ABUSIVE FATHER FORCED TO GIVE UP HIS FIVE YEAR OLD. HIS TEMPER MAKES HIM AN UNFIT PARENT. THIS OF COURSE IS A JOKE WITH MODIFIED FACTS. LAUGH NOW BECAUSE THE REST IS FACTS.

LAWS PROTECT ONLY IF THE ENFORCERS OBEY THEM

LAWS HAVE BEEN MADE TO PROTECT NEEDY AND ABUSED CHILDREN AS A MATTER OF NECCESSITY. CHILDREN ARE DEPENDENTS. THEY ARE NOT CAPABLE OF PROVIDING THEIR OWN FOOD, SHELTER, CLOTHES, DIRECTION, NECCESSITIES, AND PROVISION. THEY NEED AN ADULT TO LOOK OUT FOR THEM. THE FACT THAT CHILD ABUSE CASES NUMBER IN THE MILLIONS PER YEAR MAKES IT VERY URGENT THAT THE ADULTS THAT OVERSEE CHILDREN ARE AS IMPECABLE AS POSSIBLE IN THE MATTER OF MORAL AND ETHICAL FAIRNESS IN ADMINISTERING PROTECTION.

HOWEVER, THE FAMILY OVERSIGHT SYSTEM HAS BEEN INFECTED WITH PIRATES. PIRATES HAVE NEVER RULED ALL THE SEAS AT ONE TIME BUT THEY HAVE FLOURISHED IN MANY AREAS AROUND THE WORLD

INCLUDING AT ONE TIME, SOME OF THE HARBORS AROUND THE PROUD CITY OF NEW YORK. YES; THE LARGEST CITY IN AMERICA. ALL IT TOOK AT THAT TIME WAS A HEFTY PAYOFF TO A GOVERNOR APPOINTED BY A KING. SHOULD THE PEOPLE HAVE SHOUTED LONG LIVE THE KING OF ENGLAND OR GIVE US A FREE AMERICA? YOU GUESSED RIGHT. THEY MADE A DECISION THAT CAUSED MANY LIVES, BUT IN THE END IT BROUGHT FREEDOM TO A COUNTRY THAT TODAY IS RENOWNED AROUND THE WORLD. MOST OF US IN AMERICA HAVE NEVER HEARD THAT THE INFAMOUS PIRATE CAPTAIN KIDD ONCE USED NEW YORK CITY PORT AS HIS HEADQUARTERS. HE OBTAINED THE PRIVILEDGE THROUGH A BRIBE TO A GOVERNMENT APPOINTED PERSON.

THIS PRACTICE STILL EXISTS. CHILD REMOVAL LAWS ARE IGNORED OVER SIXTY PERCENT OF THE TIME, BUT ADOPTION LAWS ARE BEING IMPLEMENTED OVER NINETY EIGHT PERCENT OF THE TIME IN SOME AREAS AT THE TIME OF THIS WRITING. WHY? PIRATES ARE IN THE SYSTEM. OUR CHILDREN ARE BEING REMOVED ILLEGALLY AGAINST THE LAW AND BEING GIVEN AWAY TO PIRATES PROTECTED BY THEIR GOVERNORS OFTEN. OUR FREEDOMS MUST NEVER BE RELINQUISHED TO A PIRATE THAT USES OUR CONSTITUTIONAL, GOD GIVEN, BLOOD BOUGHT FAMILIES AND COURT SYSTEM TO DESTROY OUR FAMILIY FREEDOMS.

WHEN GOVERNMENT SANCTIONS REPRESSION OF ITS OWN PEOPLE, THE NATON'S DAYS ARE NUMBERED.

3. <u>A MANIPULATING FAMILY COURT</u>

A PARENT, STANDING IN A COURTROOM, REFUSED TO SIGN A STATEMENT THAT HE HAD ABANDONED HIS CHILDREN. THE LAWYER SAID TO THE JUDGE, JUST HAVE HIM SIGN THAT THE CHILDREN WERE DEPENDENTS WHEN WE PICKED THEM UP. THIS THE PARENT DID. HE THEN READ THE WORDS IN THE COURT REPORT THAT BY HIS OWN ADMISSION, HE HAD PLEADED GUILTY TO ABANDONMENT, ENDANGERMENT, FAILURE TO PROTECT, FAILURE TO PROVIDE, FAILURE TO EDUCATE, FAILURE TO PROVIDE MEDICAL AND OTHER NEEDS OF HIS CHILD. HE WAS SHOCKED. HE ASKED THE QUESTION, WHEN DID DEPENDENT, (A PERSON UNDER EIGHTEEN) EVER GRADUATE TO MEANING ALL OF THESE THINGS?

THIS PARENT FOUND THAT THE LAWS THAT WERE INTENDED TO PROTECT CHILDREN WERE AT THAT TIME AND STILL ARE TODAY, BEING TWISTED AND MANIPULATED TO LITERALLY TAKE CONTROL OF ANY PARENT OR CHILD THAT IT CHOOSES. HE FOUND THAT WHEN HE WALKED INTO THE COURTROOM, HE WAS JUST AN ORDINARY PARENT. WHEN HE WALKED OUT OF THE COURTROOM, HIS CHILD WAS IN THE CARE AND CUSTODY OF THE COURT. HIS DAILY PARENTING DUTIES WERE WRONG. HE HAD YELLED AT THE CHILD: VERBAL ABUSE: SPANKED THE CHILD: PHYSICAL ABUSE: REFUSED TO ALLOW CHILD TO VISIT FRIENDS: MENTAL ABUSE:

CHILD FELL WHILE PLAYING: CHILD ENDANGERMENT: GRANDPARENT VISITED TWO WEEKS DURING THE SUMMER: EXPOSED CHILD TO A PERSON THAT HAD A CHILD ABUSE CHARGE (UNSUBSTANTUATED), SEVERALL YEARS IN THE PAST. HIS CONCLUSION WAS AND STILL IS THAT ANY PARENT THAT PROVIDES ANY TYPE OF CONTROL OR LEADERSHIP OVER HIS FAMILY WILL NEVER BE GOOD ENOUGH TO COME OUT OF ANY SUCH COURT A VICTOR AS LONG AS ANY CHARGE MADE IS A REASON TO RULE AGAINST A PARENT.

HE FOUND THAT THE WORD DEPENDENT WAS STATED BY THE COURT AS NEGLECTED AND DEPENDENT. WEBSTERS DICTIONARY HAD BEEN TOSSED OUT OF THE COURT AND A NEW VERSION ADDED. INSIDE THE CHILDREN OR FAMILY COURT, HE HAD BECOME A LIER, VIOLENT MAN AND A CRIMINAL UNFIT TO RAISE HIS OWN FAMILY. HIS FAMILY WAS PUT ON THE AUCTION BLOCK FOR ADOPTION. NOT A DRINKER, SMOKER, DRUG USER, NO CRIMINAL RECORD BUT <u>HIS FAMILY WAS TAKEN AWAY BECAUSE A SOCIAL WORKER SAID SO ON THE STRENGTH OF ONE WORD, MISINTERPRETED BY A FAMILY COURT. THE ONE WORD WAS USED AS A SCREEN AND THE OTHER WORDS IN THE SENTENCE WERE ADDED IN THE FUTURE REFERENCES TO HIS SIGNATURE.</u> HOW CAN AN INNOCENT PERSON LOSE THEIR FAMILY IN AMERICA THE LAND OF THE FREE? HE WAS THE POOR HONEST AMERICAN WITHOUT THE MONEY TO FIGHT HIS CASE. THE ENFORCERS LAUGHED AND TOOK THEIR BRIBES, OR SHOULD I SAY THEIR SALARIES AND HIS CHILDREN.

TO ADD INSULT TO INJURY, HE HAD TO PAY FOR THE SUPPORT OF HIS CHILDREN BY ORDER OF THIS SAME COURT. IMAGINE HIS ANGER. HIS CHILDREN IN ANOTHER MAN'S HOUSE THAT HE MUST SUPPORT WHILE BEING INNOCENT OF ANY WRONG. HE WAS A PAWN OF THE CHILD PROTECTIVE SERVICE AND THE HUMAN RESOURCE WELFARE SYSTEM. <u>WHY DOES A FAMILY COURT OR A HUMAN SERVICE AGENCY FACING MILLIONS OF VALID CASES OF CHILD ABUSE YEARLY HAVE TO FABRICATE FACTS TO POESSES AN INNOCENT FAMILY'S CHILDREN?</u> VALID CASES AND NOT VALID QUOTAS SHOULD BE THE NORM IN THE CHILDREN'S AGENCIES AND THE CHILDREN'S COURTS. LAW AND ORDER ENFORCEMENT DEMANDS AN EXAMPLE OF WORTHY ENFORCERS AND RIGID, HONEST, TIGHT ROPE WALKERS AS FAR AS THE LAW IS CONCERNED. <u>WHEN AMERICA HAS OVER ONE AND A HALF MILLION (1,500,000) CHILDREN LIVING IN THE STREETS WITHOUT A HOME, WHY IS IT NECESSARY TO TARGET A QUALIFIED PARENT'S CHILD TO ADOPT OUT?</u>

4. <u>PRE APPROVED COURT APPOINTED ADOPTION ** (TWICE)</u>

A COUPLE HAD DECIDED TO PURSUE A PROFESSIONAL CAREER AND ABSTAIN FROM HAVING CHILDREN UNTIL THEY WERE IN THEIR EARLY FORTIES. WHEN THEY REACHED THEIR FORTISH YEARS, THEY CHOSE INSTEAD TO ADOPT TWO CHILDREN. THE ADOPTION AGENCY WAS GIVEN THE ORDER TO LOOK FOR A BOY AND GIRL. THEY WERE GIVEN AN AGE RANGE. THEY WANTED TWO CHILDREN THAT WERE OLD ENOUGH TO BE ALMOST SELF SUFFICIENT IN DRESSING AND FEEDING THEMSELVES, ETC. THEY WANTED THEM YOUNG ENOUGH TO GROW UP BELIEVING THEY WERE THEIR OWN CHILDREN OR THAT THEY OWED THIS COUPLE THEIR LIFETIME SUCCESS.

MARISSA WAS THE IDEAL SOURCE FOR THEIR DREAMS. MARISSA HAD LEFT HOME AT FOURTEEN YEARS OLD. SHE HAD BORN TWO CHILDREN OUT OF WEDLOCK AND WAS LIVING IN A CITY ASSISTED SHELTER. HER TWO CHILDREN'S AGES WERE A PERFECT MATCH FOR THE COUPLE. MARK WAS FOUR AND MIKAI WAS THREE YEARS OLD. NOT HAVING A PERMANENT HOME FOR HER FAMILY BECAME A REASON FOR MARISSA TO LOSE HER CHILDREN. THIS SAME EXCUSE ALSO BECAME A REASON FOR A COUPLE TO HAVE ECASTATIC JOY OVER THE

WONDERFUL NEW FAMILY THAT THEY WERE FORTUNATE ENOUGH TO ADOPT.

MARISSA'S THIRD CHILD WAS ALSO TAKEN AND GIVEN UP FOR INSTANT ADOPTION. HER THIRD CHILD WAS TAKEN FROM MARISSA AT THE HOSPITAL. AFTER THE BIRTH, MARISSA WAS NOT ALLOWED TO BRING HER SON HOME. HE WAS SENT HOME FROM THE HOSPITAL TO A WAITING ADOPTION FAMILY.

MARISA DID NOT HAVE ADDITIONAL FAMILY IN THAT CITY. SHE WENT TO THE HOMELESS SHELTER THINKING THAT THEY WERE HER FRIENDS AND THAT THEIR INTENTION WAS TO HELP HER. INSTEAD SHE FOUND A SYSTEM CONNECTION THAT CITED HER AS AN UNFIT PARENT.

HER THREE CHILDREN WERE TAKEN, NEVER TO BE RETURNED. HER SYSTEM CONNECTION MADE HER A CANDIDATE FOR ANY FUTURE ADOPTION MARKET SEARCHERS. MARISSA'S NEXT CHILD WAS ON THE ADOPTION BLOCK BEFORE HE WAS BORN. WHY? JUST BECAUSE MOTHER DID NOT HAVE A PERMANENT HOME? WHY DID A BABY HAVE TO BE TAKEN FROM THE ARMS OF A MOTHER TO BE GIVEN AWAY WHEN WE HAVE THOUSANDS OF PARENTLESS CHILDREN IN NEED OF A HOME? I CALL THIS A RUTHLESS, HEARTLESS PRACTICE THAT MUST BE STOPPED TODAY IF OUR AMERICAN FAMILIES ARE TO SURVIVE.

MARISSA'S COURT INSTILLED DAMAGE

MARISSA'S SHATTERED DREAMS WILL ALWAYS BE A HAUNTING MEMORY WITHIN HER HEART. MARISSA'S HEART OFTEN SKIPS A BEAT WHEN SHE SEES A CHILD THAT HAS FACIAL FEATURES SIMILLIR TO HER DAUGHTER MIKAI AND HER SON MARK. MARISSA NOW HAS A LIFETIME HEARTBREAK. SHE HAS A LIFETIME CLOSET OF STRIFE AND GREIF IN HER HEART. WILL SHE EVER GET OVER THIS PERSONAL TRAGEDY? NO! MARISSA WILL GET OVER THE OUTWARD SYMPTOMS, BUT THE INWARD GRIEF WILL STAY WITH MARISSA UNTIL SHE DIES. SHE WILL SPEND MANY DAYS AND NIGHTS FIGHTING THE THOUGHT OF WHERE ARE MY CHILDREN? ARE THEY BEING SENT TO BED WITH A HUG AND A PRAYER? WILL THEY WAKE UP WITH A BRIGHT SMILE AND I LOVE YOU? IT WILL SEEM AS THOUGH MARISSA HAS LOST THE USE OF HER RIGHT ARM. HER DEPRESSION AND SORROW WILL REACH THE POINT WHERE MARK AND MIKAI WILL BECOME A LIFETIME SHADOW IN HER LIFE.

ANY FUTURE CHILDREN WILL ALWAYS HAVE A MARK AND MIKAI BEHIND THEM. A LATE RETURN FROM SCHOOL, A FAILURE TO CALL HOME UPON ARRIVAL AT A FRIEND'S HOUSE, SUCH A SMALL THING AS DISAPPEARING FROM THE FRONT LAWN AND REAPEARING IN THE BACK YARD WILL TRIGGER NEAR HEART FAILURE IN MARISSA. JUST A FEW SECONDS WITHOUT PHYSICAL VISIBILITY OF HER PRESENT CHILDREN OFTEN SENDS MARRISA INTO A PANIC. HER CHILDREN ARE VISIBLY GONE BUT THEIR SPIRIT WILL ALWAYS BE WITH MARISSA. HER LIFE

AND FAMILY HAVE BEEN FOREVER CHANGED WITH A WOUND THAT REACHES TO HER VERY SOUL. A FEAR OF LOSING ANOTHER CHILD HAS LOCKED INTO HER VERY HEART AND SOUL. IT LIES DORMANT MOST OF THE TIME BUT WHEN THAT FEAR AWAKES, A FEW SECONDS SEEMS LIKE AN ETERNITY OF SORROWS FOR MARISSA. HUMAN SERVICE, WELFARE AND CHILD PROTECTIVE SERVICES HAVE COMBINED TO DESTROY ANY FUTURE HARMONY IN A STRUGLING FAMILY. HOW MANY TIMES MUST MARISSA'S STORY BE REPEATED?

5. <u>CHILDREN PRISONS ON THE MARCH</u>

SOME OF THE NAMES FOR CHILDREN PRISONS ARE KINSHIP CARE, FAMILY CARE, COUNTY GROUP CARE, CHILD PLACEMENT AGENCY, FOSTER HOME, GROUP HOME, RESIDENTIAL HOME OR RESIDENTIAL CARE, TREATMENT CENTERS, TRANSITIONAL CENTERS, ADOPTION SERVICES, HOME PLACEMENT. ALL OFFERED WITH LOVE; VERBALLY.

EVERY ATTEMPT TO SUPPRESS A GROUP'S CIVIL RIGHTS THAT IS RECORDED IN HISTORY HAS RESULTED IN VIOLENT OPPOSITION ON A MAJOR SCALE AND HAS PRODUCED THE DEATHS OF UNTOLD MILLIONS IN THE PROCESS OF THE ATTEMPTS. <u>THE SUPPRESSION OF CIVIL RIGHTS DECLARES THE SUPREMACY OF CONTROL AND THE EXERCISE OF AUTHORITY OVER ANOTHER. A MAN'S GREATEST INSTINCT TO RESIST AUTHORITY IS ALWAYS STIRRED BY DANGER OR THE THREAT OF DANGER TO HIS FAMILY.</u>

THE REJECTION OF GOD GIVEN PRINCIPLES IN MARRIAGE HAS RESULTED IN AMERICA HAVING THE HIGHEST DIVORCE RATE IN THE WORLD. PROSPERITY, IMMORALITY, AND THE FAILURE TO RESPECT EACH OTHER HAS LED TO THE OPEN PRACTICE OF DISRESPECTING HOMES BY AUTHORITIES. THE WRITTEN LAW FOR FAMILY STABILITY IS ROUTINELY BEING CAST

ASIDE AND IGNORED BY OUR HUMAN SERVICE AND FAMILY ORIENTED AGENCIES AND COURTS TOO OFTEN.

THE IDEA THAT I KNOW BETTER THAN A PARENT PERCEPTION IS TOO OFTEN INJECTED INTO THE GIVE ME YOUR CHILD FOR HOME REMOVAL EFFORTS. NO ONE IS MORE QUALIFIED TO RAISE A CHILD THAN A PARENT. WHY ARE MORE THAN SIXTY PERCENT OF THESE REMOVALS NOT FACTUALLY SUBSTANTUATED? FROM A FAMILY HOME TO A CHILDREN'S PRISON HOME IS A TRAUMATIC EXPERIENCE FOR BOTH CHILDREN AND PARENTS.

THE GOAL OF THE MARCHERS

NEBUCHADNEZZER WAS NOT CALLED A SUPPRESSOR OF CIVIL RIGHTS. HE WAS CALLED THE RULER OF THE THEN KNOWN WORLD. THE CIVIL RIGHTS OF THE THEN KNOWN WORLD PERISHED IN A SEA OF BLOOD BEFORE THE MARCHING FEET OF THIS WORLD RULER.

HISTORY IS ABLE TO RECOUNT IN A FEW WORDS THE GLORY OF RULERSHIP. LET YOUR KNOWLEDGE SEE THIS RULE AS IT WAS. SEE THOUSANDS DYING BY THE SWORD. SEE THE ARMIES MARCHING WHILE CREATING CRYING WIDOWS, ORPHANED CHILDREN AND WOUNDED MEN WITH SEVERED ARMS AND LEGS. VISION MEN AND WOMEN DYING IN DEFENSE OF THEIR RIGHT TO LIVE WITHOUT FORCED SERVITUDE.

NEBUCHADNEZZER DID NOT HAVE TO RULE OTHER NATIONS. HE CHOSE TO RULE OTHER NATIONS. HE USED FORCE WITH A SWORD AND SPEAR TO DO IT. A RIVER OF BLOOD FOLLOWED IN THE WAKE OF HIS MARCHING ARMY. TODAY AMERICA'S CHILD REMOVAL PROGRAM HAS NOT CREATED A SEA OF BLOOD BUT WE HAVE CERTAINLY LEFT A SEA OF BROKEN FAMILIES. BROKEN IN BOTH MENTAL, AND PHYSICAL HEALTH, BROKEN IN FAMILY RULE, DIRECTION, AMBITION, DESIRE AND SUCCESS. WE HAVE CREATED AN ARMY OF UNWILLING CITIZENS THAT CAN NEVER SUPPORT A CENTRAL PROGRAM WITH ENTHUSIASM OR FULL COOPERATION.

MILITARY GENIUS OR HEARTLESS FAMILY RIGHTS KILLER

ALEXANDER THE GREAT WAS NOT CALLED AN OPPRESSOR OF THE NATIONS THAT HE CONQUERED. HE WAS MORE WELL KNOWN FOR HIS BATTLE GENIUS AND THE TEARS THAT HE SHED WHEN THERE WERE NO MORE NATIONS TO BE CONQUERED. EVERY NATION HE CONQUERED GAVE UP THEIR CIVIL RIGHTS AT THE EDGE OF THE SWORD.

THE WORLD BOWED TO ITS CONQUEROR IN THE MIDST OF THE GRAVES OF ITS SONS AND DAUGHTERS. CIVIL RIGHTS WERE LOST IN THE HEAT OF SLAUGHTER. AS MILLIONS LOST THEIR LIVES, HISTORY RECORDED THE MARCH OF THE VICTORS. HISTORY IGNORED THE DEATH OF THE MILLIONS DURING THE MARCH. EVERY

ARMY THAT AROSE TO CHALLENGE THE THREAT TO THEIR CERTAIN UNALIENABLE RIGHTS TO BE FREE FROM THE REPRESSION AND DOMINANCE OF THEIR FELLOW MEN ENDED IN DEFEAT. THEIR LIFE, LIBERTY, AND THE PURSUIT OF HAPPINESS DIED. THEY LEFT THEIR DEAD ON A BATTLEFIELD. THEIR ONLY HONOR IN DEATH WAS THE KNOWLEDGE THAT THEY HAD TRIED TO DEFEND THEIR FAMILY AGAINST A GOVERNMENT OPPRESSOR.

THEIR FAMILIES WERE GIVEN TO OTHERS: OVER THEIR DEAD BODIES. OTHER MEN MOVED INTO THEIR HOMES: OVER THEIR DEAD BODIES. WERE THEY LOSERS? NO. ONLY MEN THAT SAID MY HOME IS SACRED. MY CHILDREN ARE MY CHARGE. I WILL DIE IF NECESSARY. I WILL GIVE MY ALL FOR MY FAMILY. THEIR RIGHTS IS PRECIOUS. THEY DIED FOR THE VALUE OF THEIR FREEDOM AND CIVIL RIGHTS.

AMERICA BEGAN WITH SUCH A SPIRIT. WHERE IS THE LOVE FOR FAMILY RIGHTS AND FAMILY FREEDOM TO RAISE OUR FAMILIES IN THE LIFE, LIBERTY AND PURSUIT OF HAPPINESS THAT OUR CONSTITUTION SO NOBLY CALLS FOR? HAVE WE LOST OUR SPIRIT FOR FREEDOM? OR MAYBE WE JUST DON'T KNOW WHAT OUT OF HOME PLACEMENT ENTAILS.

MAYBE WE HAVE NOT YET GRASPED THE MEANING OF LONELINESS, FEAR, DEPRESSION, AND TERROR, FOR A CHILD SEPARATED FROM HIS FAMILY. THIS IS NOT LIKE BEING AFRAID OF THE DARK OR NIGHTMARES. THIS IS A LIVING NIGHTMARE IN THE DARK FOR A CHILD.

500 YEARS OF GLORIOUS RULE OR 500 YEARS CIVIL RIGHTS OPPRESSION OF OTHER NATIONS FAMILY FREEDOMS

ROME IS REMEMBERED AS A NATION WHO NEEDED NO WALLS BUT THAT OF ITS ARMY WITH THEIR SWORD AND SHIELDS. YET THEIR STRENGTH WAS BUILT ON THE BLOOD OF THE FAMILIES WHOSE CIVIL RIGHTS THEY DESTROYED. THEIR ARMY WAS NOTED FOR SUCCESS, AS EACH MAN WAS RESPONSIBLE FOR DOMINATING THE SIX FOOT SQUARE AREA IN FRONT OF HIM.

YET EACH MAN THAT FELL IN DEATH BEFORE THIS ONSLAUGHT WAS DYING FOR HIS CIVIL RIGHTS. THE RIGHT TO LIVE AS A FREE MAN IN HIS OWN HOUSE, IN HIS OWN CITY, IN HIS OWN COUNTRY. THE RIGHT TO BE FREE TO MAKE HIS OWN DECISIONS THE RIGHT TO ATTEND HIS OWN CHURCH, START HIS OWN BUSINESS, EDUCATE HIS OWN CHILDREN, CHOOSE THE LAND FOR THEIR OWN FARM WITHOUT GOVERNMENT INTERFERENCE. THEY DIED FOR FAMILY FREEDOM.

STILL THE LUXERY OF SUCCESS OFTEN FORGETS THAT THE ROAD TO SUCCESS ALSO CARRIES THE UNBRIDLED SEEDS OF FAILURE. REVENGE, JEALOUSY, ENVY, ANGER, RESENTMENT, AND OTHER BY PRODUCTS OF VICTORY WILL ALWAYS NIP AT THE HEELS OF THE VICTORS. IF LEFT UNTENDED THE GRASS WILL OVER RUN ANY GARDEN. THE DESIRE TO BE FREE FROM TYRANY NEVER LEAVES THE HEART OF MANKIND. NO AMOUNT OF WEEDING CAN EVER GUARANTEE A WEED

FREE GARDEN. MAN WAS CREATED TO BE FREE AND FREE INDEED. NO AMOUNT OF PERSECUTION OR EFFORT WILL EVER FREE MANKIND OF THE DESIRE TO BE FREE FROM OPPRESSION OF HIMSELF AND HIS FAMILY.

THE KNOWLEDGE THAT EVERY MAN'S FAMILY CAN BE OVER RUN AT WILL BY AN AMERICAN AGENCY ESTABLISHED BY OUR GOVERNMENT IS WORSE THAN A RUNAWAY ATOM BOMB. THIS KNOWLEDGE TESTS EVERY MOTHER'S LOVE AND EVERY FATHER'S RESPONSIBILITY.

GOD IS THE GIVER OF LIFE. WE CANNOT SURVIVE WITHOUT HIS GIFT. STILL THE ALMIGHTY GOD AND THE CREATOR OF THE UNIVERSE ALLOWS US O MAKE

THE DECISION OF WHETHER WE WILL SUBMIT TO HIM OR NOT. ONLY MEN WITH A TWISTED MIND AND LACK OF RESPECT AND RECOGNITION OF THEIR FELLOW EARTH CITIZENS COULD REVEL IN FORCED SUBJECTION TO ANOTHER MAN. FAMILY CIVIL RIGHTS MUST BE KEPT FREE IN AMERICA.

6. <u>BLIND SPOTS DANGEROUS CATARACTS</u>

A POSITION THAT IS GAINED BY THE DESTRUCTION OF A NATION'S CIVIL RIGHTS, MUST CONTINUE TO DESTROY THOSE CIVIL RIGHTS IN ORDER TO MAINTAIN THAT POSITION. THE HIGHER A TYRANT RISES, THE MORE CIVIL RIGHTS HE ABUSES. EVERY ABUSED MAN, WOMAN, OR CHILD IS A SHADOWY THREAT AT EACH TURN OF THE ROAD FOR THE TYRANT.

EVEN IN THE HALLS OF THE ROMAN SENATE, BRUTUS STOOD UP THINKING HE WAS FIGHTING AND KILLING FOR RIGHTS AND JUSTICE. HE WAS NOT A SOLDIER. HE WAS A SENATOR. HE WAS A MAN RESPONSIBLE FOR THE LAWS OF THE LAND. HE AROSE FROM AMONG THE HIGHEST OFFICE IN THE LAND WITH A SWORD IN HIS HAND. HE FELT THAT CEASER HAD GONE TOO FAR. THE CORRUPTION THAT HAD TRAMPLED THE MASS OF PEOPLE IN MANY COUNTRIES AND ESTABLISHED AN ELITE LEADERSHIP HAD NOW BEGUN TO TRAMPLE THE TOP LEADERS. ONE OF THOSE SEEDS OF FAILURE THAT HAD BEEN NIPPING AT THE HEELS OF THE NATIONAL LEADERS THROUGHOUT THEIR SUCCESS CLIMB HAD NOW CAUGHT UP WITH CEASER.

BRUTUS, A FRIEND AND FELLOW LEADER, NOW OFFERED HIS SWORD TO KILL CEASER. WHEN ROME FELT SECURE IN ITS POWER AND AUTHORITY THE STRONG

FELL AND SO DID HISTORY. ROME AT THE PEAK OF ITS POWER WAS READY TO CHANGE AND BECOME FULLY RESPECTABLE TOWARD ITS GOVERNING BODIES BUT IT WAS TOO LATE. TOO MANY HAD DIED TO REACH THIS PLACE OF POWER. THE WORLD LEADER HAD WAITED TOO LONG. CEASER DIED AT THE HAND OF HIS FELLOW LEADERS AND GAVE HISTORY A NEW TASK.

HISTORY'S NEW TASK WAS TO REWRITE ITSELF ABOUT THE RISE OF ROME AND INCLUDE THE STORY OF ITS FALL. HISTORY WILL WRITE THAT ROME FELL BECAUSE THE GOVERNMENT BECAME CORRUPT. LIFE WAS NO LONGER IMPORTANT. A MAN, WOMAN OR CHILD COULD BE KILLED IN THE ARENA AND IT WAS ONLY A GOOD LAUGH OR SHOW. THIS WAS THEIR PRIME TIME TV. LIFE AND CIVIL RIGHTS, WHAT WAS THAT? IN ROME, IT WAS DEATH TO THOSE I DON'T LIKE. THE SLAVE, CHRISTIAN, PRISONER, THE POOR died.

NO RESPECT, NO ORDER, NO NATION

THE RESPECT FOR LIFE WAS GONE. SO WAS THE NATION. THE INCREDIBLE LOSS OF THE AMERICAN FAMILY CIVIL RIGHTS DECLARES THAT CHAOS IS KNOCKING ON OUR DOOR. WITHOUT INSTANT CORRECTION OUR CEASER IS ABOUT TO DIE. WHO THEN WILL BE CAPABLE TO LEAD OUR GREAT NATION? CEASER'S DEATH OCCURRED IN THE SENATE OF THE WORLD'S MOST POWERFUL NATION.

OPEN DEFIANCE OF EQUALITY AND JUSTICE COMMON AT THE BOTTOM OF SOCIETY WILL SOON REACH THE TOP. THE BOTTOM IS THE FOUNDATION. THE TOP CANNOT STAND IF THERE IS NO FOUNDATION. DISRESPECT, ACCUSATIONS, AND FINGER POINTING IS EXTREMELY RAMPANT AMONG OUR HIGHEST ELECTED LEADERS. DISBELIEF AND LACK OF CONFIDENCE IN PARENTAL LEADERSHIP IS BEING HEAVILY CULTIVATED AMONG OUR FAMILIES AND HOME INVASION IS BECOMING A WAY OF LIFE. HOW LONG WILL IT TAKE OUR NATION TO FALL INTO A PATTERN WHERE ALL AUTHORITY IS BEING REJECTED OTHER THAN OUR OWN? THIS INVASION TOUCHES EVERY HOME. EVERY POOR HOME HAS ALREADY BECOME WARY OF APPOINTED AUTHORITIES. HOW LONG WILL IT TAKE FOR THE AVENGE YOURSELF VIGILANTE SPIRIT TO TAKE CONTROL IN AMERICAN HOMES, FAMILIES, AND CITIES?

AN OPEN ASSAULT WITHOUT FEAR OF LEADERS

AN OPEN ASSAULT ON FAMILY PARENTAL LEADERSHIP HAS BEGAN HERE IN AMERICA. OPEN ASSAULT ON OUR FAMILIES AND THE KNOWLEDGE THAT OUR LEADERS ARE NOT MOVED TO STOP THE UNJUST ASSAULT BY A FEDERALLY BACKED SOCIAL SERVICE HAS SPARKED A NATIONWIDE REBELLION AGAINST THIS PRACTICE OF UNJUSTIFIED HOME REMOVAL OF OUR CHILDREN. WHEN OVER THREE HUNDRED THOUSAND (300,000) INCIDENTS OCCUR IN ONE YEAR, IT IS A SIGN THAT OUR CRISIS HAS ALREADY BEGAN. PREOCCUPATION

WITH FOREIGN EFFORTS HAS KEPT OUR OWN LOCAL CRISIS OUT OF THE NEWS MEDIA. AS ONE MAN PUT IT, SOME THINGS WE DO NOT WANT TO BE KNOWN. IF THE GENERAL PUBLIC BECOMES AWARE OF IT, WE CAN BE FLOODED WITH SIMILAR PROBLEMS.

<u>OUT OF OVER FOUR HUNDRED THIRTY LEADERS OF AMERICA'S LEGISLATIVE BODY, LESS THAN TEN WERE CONCERNED AS TO THIS HOME REMOVAL BEING AN AMERICA PROBLEM. CAN A LEGISLATURE THAT MAKES THE LAWS FOR THE WORLD'S GREATEST NATION NOT KNOW THAT MOST OUT OF HOME FAMILY PLACEMENTS THAT ARE NOT SUBSTANTUATED WITH SOUND FACTS SHOULD NOT BE USED UNJUSTLY AGAINST OUR PEOPLE? WITH THE FULL KNOWLEDGE THAT OVER SIXTY PERCENT OF HOME REMOVAL OF CHILDREN IN AMERICA IS UNFOUNDED AS TO THE REMOVAL REASON, IT IS ASTOUNDING THAT LESS THAN TEN WERE WILLING TO VOICE A WORD TO AID IN CORRECTION OTHER THAN TO SAY THAT THIS IS NOT MY ELECTED JOB.</u>

THE FAMILY IS OUR FOUNDATION. AMERICA CANNOT STAND WITHOUT STRONG FAMILY PROTECTION. IF THERE IS NO FAMILY CONTROL; THERE CAN BE NO NATION. A PERSON IN OFFICE THAT CARES NOT ABOUT FAMILY LAW AND ITS MISUSE BY THE OVERSEERS OF IT WILL STAND BY AND FIDDLE WHILE AMERICA BURNS. TEN OUT OF OVER FOUR HUNDRED LAWMAKERS THAT WERE NOTIFIED IS NOT ENOUGH VOICES FOR AMERICAN FAMILY SUPPORT. IF A LAWMAKER IS AFRAID TO SPEAK UP FOR THE AMERICAN FAMILY, WHO WILL?

GIVE ME A PARENT THAT WILL STAND AS A PARENT AND HISTORY WILL GIVE THE WORLD ANOTHER LEADER OF COMPASSION, JUSTICE, AND HONOR.

IT IS RIGHT TO SPEAK FOR A SET AREA OF VOTERS BUT IT IS WRONG TO BE WILLINGLY BLIND OR SILENT TO ANY PROBLEM THAT ARISES OR EXPANDS ON A NATIONAL SCALE. WHY? TODAY IT IS MY NEIGHBORS. TOMORROW IT IS YOUR NEIGHBORS. THE NEXT DAY IT IS YOU. LEADERS SHOULD NOT BE AFRAID TO BE LEADERS IN RIGHT. LAWS ARE GREAT. WHETHER WE DRIVE, VOTE, HUNT, SWIM OR OVERSEE FAMILIES. LET THEM BE FAIR AND JUSTLY APPLIED. OUR HOMES ARE SACRED. LET FAMILY OVERSIGHT BE JUST AS SACRED.

YESTERDYAY MINORITIES ** TODAY EVERY FAMILY

CIVIL RIGHTS VIOLATIONS HAVE ALWAYS EXISTED IN AMERICA. WE HAVE ALWAYS BEEN A NATION OF IMMIGRANTS. THE BLACK AMERICAN HAS ALWAYS BEEN THE MOST TARGETED BECAUSE HE IS THE MOST VISIBLE. THE BLACK AMERICAN MALE HAS BEEN THE MOST FEARED AND THE MOST TARGETED FOR NATIONAL GENOCIDE IN AMERICA BECAUSE HE ALSO POSSESS THE ABILITY TO BE THE MOST SUCCESSFUL PERSON IN ANY AREA THAT HE SO CHOOSE. HE HAS THE ABILITY TO EXCELL IN THE FACE OF ALL ODDS IF HE CHOOSES TO DO SO. HE POSSESSES THE CHARACHTERISTICS AND GENES IN HIS BODY OF EVERY NATION THAT AMERICA IS COMPOSED OF. HE IS THE EXAMPLE OF THE INTEGRATED

AMERICAN. IF LEFT ALONE, AND ALLOWED TO DEVELOP HIS IDEAS, AND IDEALS HE WILL BECOME THE MOST BRILLIANT, AND CAPABLE SET OF MEN IN AMERICA FROM SCIENCE TO EDUCATION, MEDICAL, SPORTS, AND STYLES.

THIS KNOWLEDGE IN THE HANDS OF HISTORIANS HAVE MADE THIS GROUP OF MEN THE MOST MANIPULATED GROUP OF MEN IN AMERICA SINCE THE END OF SLAVERY. FROM 1865 TO 1895 WAS THE GREATEST JUMP IN THE ECONOMIC AND CULTURAL SUCCESS OF THIS GROUP IN ITS AMERICAN HISTORY. THIS THIRTY-YEAR SPAN HAS BEEN THE MEASURE OF SUCCESS THAT HAS STIRRED THE FEAR OF LEADERSHIP LOSS BY MANY IN AMERICA, ESPECIALLY HATE ORIENTATED GROUPS. IT IS ALSO THE MEASUREMENT THAT HAS STIRRED THE EFFORT TO SCATTER AND DIVIDE THIS GROUP ABOVE ANY OTHER GROUP IN AMERICA.

IN SPITE OF DENIAL OF JOBS, EDUCATION, MEDICINE AND VOTING RIGHTS, WITH RAPES, VIOLENCE, MURDER, AND RAMPANT INTIMIDATION, THEY WENT FORWARD AND PROSPERED. THEIR PROGRESS WAS SLOWED BUT NEVER STOPED BY A COMBINATION OF THE SEPARATE BUT EQUAL DECISION FROM THE COURTS AND THE UNITING OF THE SOUTHERN POLITICAL COALITION WITH TWO SUCCESIVE PRESIDENTS. WHAT POLITICS AND REGIONALISM HAS FAILED TO DO TO THESE MINORITIES IN THE PAST, IT SEEMS THAT OUR CHILD AND FAMILY ORIENTATED LAWS AND ORGANIZATIONS HAVE BEGUN TO DO TO EVERY AMERICAN FAMILY.

EVERY AMERICAN HOME IS IN THE PATH OF FAMILY CONTROL.

THE TRAGEDY IS THAT AT PRESENT OVER SIXTY PERCENT OF HOME FAMILY CHILD REMOVALS IS WITHOUT VALID PROOF, OR REASONS. THE EVEN GREATER TRAGEDY IS THAT <u>WE HAVE CLOSED OUR EYES TO A DICTATORSHIP PRACTICE THAT CAN EVENTUALLY CONTROL ALL AMERICAN FAMILY HOMES.</u>

THE AMERICAN INDIANS HAVE ALWAYS BEEN THE MOST RESTRICTED FOR THEY HAVE BEEN COMMITTED TO SET PIECES OF LAND CALLED RESERVATIONS. THEIR RESERVATIONS HAVE BEEN SET IN THE WORST OF THE LAND AND STAND AS A SHAME AND DISGRACE TO A COUNTRY THAT LIKES TO PRIDE ITSELF IN FREEDOM AND EQUALITY. THE DAY THAT THE NATIVE AMERICAN IS ALLOWED TO BE A PART OF HIS ORIGINAL LAND WITHOUT THE PREJUDICE OF BEING CONFINED TO HIS RESERVATION ISLAND IS THE DAY THAT AMERICE WILL HAVE TRULY BECOME A FREE NATION FOR ITS PEOPLE. THESE CIVIL RIGHTS HAVE BEEN TRAMPLED ON FOR YEARS.

7. __TO FORGET IS TO FAIL__

__TODAY AMERICA IS FACING ITS GREATEST DANGER.__
__EVERY HOME AND FAMILY IS BEING THREATENED.__
WE HAVE FORGOTTEN THAT HISTORY SHOULD HAVE
TAUGHT US A LESSON. HALLOWEEN SHOULD REMIND
US THAT WHEN THE DRUIDS ASKED A HOME TO GIVE UP
TO THEM A DAUGHTER, IT WAS TO KILL HER IN A HUMAN
SACRAFICE. THIS WAS ASSOCIATED WITH RITUAL KILLING
AND INSTILLING FEAR INTO NOT ONLY THE TARGETED
CASTLE BUT ALSO THE ENTIRE POPULATION.

WHAT DOES YOUR HOME INVASION AND
CHILDREN PRISONS MEAN? __TOTAL CONTROL OF YOUR__
__FAMILY OR ANY FAMILY. TO GIVE UP YOUR CHILD, YOU__
__GIVE UP YOUR DREAMS, HOPES, AMBITIONS, EDUCATION,__
__AND PREPARATION FOR LIFE FOR THAT CHILD. YOU__
__END YOUR FAMILY HERITAGE OR FUTURE. THAT CHILD__
__REPRESENTS YOU IN THE FUTURE.__

__TO FORGET IS TO LOSE FAMILY HONOR AND RESPECT__

SCOTLAND AND ITS MEDEVIAL LAW SHOULD
HAVE TAUGHT US THAT WHEN A HOME CAN BE INVADED
WITH THE HELP OF A GOVERNMENT LAW THAT NO
WIFE OR CHILD IS SAFE. A RULER COULD DEFILE THE

FEMALES AND ANY HUSBAND OR MAN THAT OBJECTED WAS KILLED WITHOUT REMORSE.

SO FAR, OUR WIVES HAVE BEEN SPARED ALL EXCEPT THE HEARTACHE AND SORROW OF LOSING HER CHILDREN AND BEING SILENCED SO SHE CANNOT FILE A MEANINGFUL PROTEST. THIS IS NOT SO WITH OUR DAUGHTERS. THE SEXUAL ABUSE OR SHOULD I SAY SEXUAL ACTIVITY OF OUR GIRLS IS BASICALLY OUT OF CONTROL WITHIN OUR FOSTER HOME SYSTEM. WHO HOLDS THE SYSTEM ACCOUNTABLE?

12 YEAR OLD GIRL

AT THE TIME OF THIS WRITING OF THIS CHAPTER** 12YEAR OLD GIRL

ONE YEAR IN OUT OF HOME PLACEMENT FOSTER CARE. ABUSED SEXUALLY ** ABUSED PHYSICALLY ** ABUSED RACIALLY ** THREATENED AND INTIMIDATED BY BOTH FOSTER PARENTS AND FOSTER CHILDREN ** RUN AWAY ** RETURNED TO SYSTEM ** SEVERAL SCHOOL SUSPENSIONS ** BECAME DRUG USER INSIDE SYSTEM ** THIRD RUNAWAY REACHED HER PARENTS HOME. NOW A TEACHER, WIFE, AND SINGER AFTER REHAB.

15-YEAR-OLD GIRL

ONE YEAR IN OUT OF HOME PLACEMENT FOSTER CARE. RAPED FIRST WEEK BY IN SYSTEM GIRLS *** RAPED

BY MEN *** RAPED BY WOMEN *** RAPED BY GIRLS *** BECAME DRUG USER INSIDE SYSTEM *** BECAME ALCOHOL USER INSIDE SYSTEM *** RUN AWAY SEVERAL TIMES *** ALWAYS RETURNED TO SYSTEM *** FORCED PROSTITUTION SEVERAL TIMES INSIDE YSTEM **** RELEASED AT 18 YRS OLD. **** NOW OUT OF CONTROL ADULT.

INSIDE SYSTEM

THIS IS NOT MEDEVIAL SCOTLAND. THIS IS AMERICA FOSTER CARE OUT OF HOME PLACEMENT SYSTEM ** THE BAD PART IS THAT IN BOTH OF THESE CASES A QUALIFIED PARENT AND GRANDPARENT WAS AVAILABLE. WHY ARE OUR GIRLS NOT BEING PROTECTED OR THE SYSTEM NOT BEING HELD ACCOUNTABLE? TODAY IT IS THESE TWO GIRLS PLUS MANY MORE. TOMORROW IT WILL BE YOUR GIRLS.

TO FORGET ** IS INDISCRIMINATE, VIOLENCE.

DISRESPECT

THE BROWN SHIRTS YOUTH ORGANIZATION PRIOR TO WORLD WAR TWO SHOULD HAVE TAUGHT US THAT NOT ONLY A PERSON'S HOME BUT THEIR BUSINESS AND LIFE ITSELF WAS AT STAKE WHEN A HOME CAN BE INVADED AT WILL WITH GOVERNMENT APPROVAL. THE FREE REIGN OF FEAR, TERROR, INTIMIDATION, DEATH,

LOOTING, AND VIOLENCE SPARKED BY THIS GROUP HAS LEFT A HORRIBLE MARK UPON OUR WORLD. IT BECAME EXTREMLY PLAIN TO EVERY OUTSIDE VIEWER OF THEIR ACTIONS AGAINST THE POPULACE AND THOSE OF US THAT ARE JUNIOR HISTORIANS THAT A NATION CAN ONLY DETERIATE AND NEVER EXCELL WHEN SUCH CONDITION EXIST WITHIN A NATION. WE SAW THIS IN GERMANY AND HISTORY.

FEAR, INTIMIDATION AND HATRED ARE ALWAYS INSTANT BY PRODUCTS OF HOME INVASION REMOVAL OF CHILDREN. THIS FEAR EXTENDS FARTHER THAN THE IMMEDIATE HOME. IT DESTROYS THE RESPECT FOR THE NUMBER ONE TEACHING AUTHORITY IN THE LAND. <u>IT IS THE PARENT THAT IS EXPECTED TO TEACH RESPECT FOR THE LAW, PROPERTY, RIGHTS OF OTHERS, WORK RULES, RELIGIONS, ETC. HOME REMOVAL WITHOUT JUST CAUSE DESTROYS TOO MUCH OF THE FAMILY FOUNDATION. IT MUST BE ** NO SOLID PROOF ** NO REMOVAL** FORTY PERCENT RIGHT IS NOT ENOUGH</u>

<u>TO FORGET MEANS WORLD WIDE CHAOS &</u>

<u>DESTRUCTION</u>

THE NAZI PRACTICE OF HOME INVASION BEGAN AMONG THE JEWS WITH JEWS WEARING MANDATORY STARS OR BADGES AS AN ETHNIC IDENTITY. THIS OPPRESION OF FAMILY CIVIL RIGHTS CONTINUED TO THE GHETTOS OF GERMANY AS LIVING QUARTERS. IT

PROGRESSED TO TRAINS DESTINED FOR SLAVE LABOR DEATH CAMPS. THE TERM, FINAL SOLUTION, FOR THE JEWS, MEANT DEATH FOR THOSE THAT THE REGIME DID NOT LIKE. AUSCHWITZ WAS NOT A RETIREMENT HOME WITH A SWIMMING POOL AND JACUZZI. IT WAS A DEATH CAMP FOR EVERY JEW THAT WAS SENT TO IT OR ARRIVED THERE BY ACCIDENT. SIX MILLLION JEWS HAVE BEEN HEARD OF CONTINUALLY AS BEING A TOTAL OF THE JESISH HOLOCCUST. SILENCE DOES NOT STOP THE ATROCIOUS COUNT.THE JEWISH NATION HAS SAID NEVER AGAIN. WE WILL REMEMBER A PARTIAL COUNT OF THE CRIMES BECAUSE THEY WERE THE JEWISH PEOPLE AND WE WILL NEVER LET IT HAPPEN AGAIN.

STILL THE NUMBER OF ACTUAL VICTEMS OF THIS NAZI LED, ETHNIC CLEANSING, AND SLAUGHTER ACCORDING TO A PARTIAL RESEARCH OF HISTORY IS NEARER TO TWENTY TWO MILLION. IT INCLUDED THE SICK, DISEASED, DISABLED, THE ETHNIC AND STRANGERS THAT DID NOT FIT THE PURE RACE PATTERN THAT HITLER HAD ESTABLISHED FOR GERMANY AT THAT TIME. ANY GROUP GRANTED FREE ACCESS OR ENTRY TO ANY HOME BY AUTHORITIES WHILE THE PARENTS OR FAMILY ARE FORCED TO STAND IDLY BY WITH HANDS TIED IS A KEYHOLE PICTURE OF TOTAL TYRANNY. <u>AMERICA CANNOT AFFORD TO SET UP A PANZER GROUP (AUTHORITIES) TO INVADE OUR HOMES UNDER CODE NAME FAMILY CONTROL CENTER</u>.

UNLESS IT IS STOPPED BY A UNITED PEOPLE IN PROTECTION OF THEIR HOMES, NOT ONE HOME,

BUT ALL HOMES AND OUR DEMOCRACY IS OVER. THE DESTRUCTION OF CIVIL RIGHTS OFTEN BEGINS VERY SMALL. STILL THE END IS THE SAME. THE VANQUESHED IS TRAMPLED UNDER FOOT *** THE STRONG IS HUMILIATED AND BROKEN *** THE DEFIANT IS HUMBLED *** AND THE UNCONQUERABLE IS SLAUGHTERED OPENLY AS A LESSON TO THE MASSES. FREEDOM WITHIN OUR HOMES MUST NOT BE SURRENDERED WITHOUT PROVEN GUILT. HISTORY HAS SHOWN THE END OF SUCH A PRACTICE. THE <u>ETHNIC MINORITY AND THE STRONGLY RELIGIOUS</u> ARE USUALLY THE FIRST TARGETS AND THE MOST PERSECUTED.

TIME TRAVELERS TO THE PAST (FAMILY SUPPRESSION

HOME INVASION FOR THE REMOVAL OF CHILDREN FROM PARENTS REMINDS ME OF AMERICAN HISTORY DURING THE SLAVE TRADE. IT WAS AN AMERICAN PRACTICE TO SEPARATE TRIBAL SLAVES FROM AFRICA TO PREVENT UNITY AND REBELLION. SLAVE FAMILIES WERE OFTEN SOLD AND SEPARATED FOR THE SAME REASON. NO REGARD WAS SHOWN FOR ANY SLAVE FAMILY. UNITY AND HARMONY AMONG SLAVE FAMILIES WAS NOT FOSTERED NOR ENCOURAGED OR CONDONED EXCEPT IN ISOLATED CASES AMONG SLAVE OWNERS. <u>TOTAL DISREGARD FOR THE LAW OF FAMILY UNITY AND CIVIL RIGHTS AMONG SLAVES WAS THE ORDER OF THE DAY.</u> IT HAS BEEN REPORTED THAT AS HIGH AS TEN THOUSAND SLAVES A YEAR WAS BROUGHT INTO SOME SOUTHERN STATES DURING THIS PERIOD OF SUPPRESSION OF SLAVE

RIGHTS AND FREEDOMS. TODAY WE DO NOT CALL THE ACCELARATING FAMILY INVASION A MODERN DAY SLAVE MOVEMENT.

WHAT SHOULD WE CALL IT? THE BLOODIEST WAR IN AMERICAN HISTORY PUT BROTHER AGAINST BROTHER, SON AGAINST FATHER, AND STATE AGAINST STATE. WHY WAS THIS WAR FOUGHT? TO REUNITE A <u>PORTION OF A NATION THAT HAD DECREED THAT DENIAL OF A FAMILIES RIGHTS WAS LEGAL AND FINANCIALLY PROSPEROUS.</u> WHAT WAS THIS WAR CALLED? THE AMERICAN CIVIL WAR. WHAT DO I CALL THE PRESENT DAY HOME INVASION AND SUPRESSSION OF FAMILY RIGHTS AND FREEDOMS? I CALL IT A RETURN TO FAMILY CIVIL RIGHTS DENIAL; I CALL IT PSEUDO SLAVERY. A RETURN TO CONSTITUTIONAL DENIAL OF FREEDOM FOR ALL AMERICANS. SLAVERY DID NOT BEGIN AS A NATION WIDE SYSTEM. YET IT SPREAD TO SOW HATRED, BLOODSHED, SORROW AND DIVISION THROUGH OUT OUR NATION. THIS WAR HAS LEFT A STAIN THAT WILL TARNISH AMERICA THROUGH OUT AMERICAN EXISTENCE.

<u>TODAY THE SIXTY PERCENT OF UNSUBSTANTUATED CHILDREN REMOVED FROM THEIR PARENTS HOMES AND THE PLACING OF PARENTS ON PAROLE, WITH THEIR CHILDREN MONITERED AS PRISONERS AND COUNTED AS CRIMINALS IF THEY RUN AWAY HAS AN ARM THAT REACHES ALL ACROSS AMERICA.</u> <u>WHY HAS THE HUMAN RESOURCE AGENCY OR THE CHILDREN PROTECTIVE AGENCY, OR RELATED FAMILY CONCERN GROUPS BEEN</u>

GIVEN FREE RANGE <u>WITHOUT THE NECESSITY TO</u> <u>OBEY THE CHILDREN'S CODE OR THE CIVIL RIGHTS</u> <u>CODE?</u> THESE CODES ARE THE SAME IN EVERY STATE ACROSS AMERICA. DO WE HAVE A BREACH IN AMERICAN CONSTITUTIONAL LAW OR ITS ENFORCEMENT? WHICH AGENCY IN AMERICA IS ABOVE THE LAW? A NEW STAIN HAS ARISEN IN THIS CENTURY.

THE PATTERN IS HERE **** SHUT THE GATE

CHECK YOUR HISTORY BOOKS. WE HAVE AN INVASION OF HOMES IN AMERICA. WHEN WILL THE SIXTY (60%) PERCENT OF UNPROVEN OR UNSUBSTANTUATED HOME REMOVALS OF CHILDREN RISE TO ONE HUNDRED (100%) PERCENT UNNECCESARY EVIDENCE NEEDED TO INVADE, HOLD, REMOVE, OR CONVICT AS LONG AS PARENTS OR CHILDREN ARE INVOLVED? IT IS A DIFFERENT DAY. IT IS THE SAME GAME. IT IS A DIFFERENT NAME. <u>THE FATHER IS BEING TERMINATED. THE MOTHER IS</u> <u>BEING ELIMINATED. THE CHLDREN ARE BEING GIVEN</u> <u>TO STRANGERS FOR RETRAINING.</u>

THOUSANDS OF HOMES HAVE BEEN ENTERED AND CONTROLLED BY A COUNTY, STATE, OR GOVERNMENT AGENCY AND THOUSANDS HAVE BEEN TOLD THAT THEY CANNOT BE A PARENT. THE THOUSANDS HAVE BEEN KEPT ISOLATED IN KNOWLEDGE AND DO NOT KNOW THAT THEY ARE NOT ALONE BUT ARE PART OF A FAMILY PLAN THAT INVOLVES MILLIONS. THE HUMAN SERVICE WELFARE AGENCY AND RELATED FAMILY CONCERN GROUPS ACROSS AMERICA HAVE TOO OFTEN

BECOME NOTED AS FAMILY DESTROYERS INSTEAD OF FAMILY UNIFIERS BY FOLLOWING A PATTERN THAT HAS ALIENATED, SCATTERED, AND DIVIDED MILLIONS OF FAMILIES IN THE PAST. FAMILIES MAKE UP OUR NATION OF AMERICA. DO <u>WE LISTEN TO HISTORY AND GROW OR WATCH HISTORY AND PERISH</u>?

8. <u>THE SINGLE FAMILY ** IMMORALITY TO TRAGEDY</u>

A FEW YEARS AGO WHILE DOING RESEARCH ON THE BOOK AFDC CADILLAC AND CHILD SUPPORT, I WAS STRUCK BY THE STATISTICS OF OUR NATION'S CAPITOL. WASHINGTON D.C. THE CRIME RATE FOR THE CAPITOL OF THE WORLD WAS HORRENDOUS. MORE OMINOUS TO ME WAS THE BIRTH RATE. MORE WOMEN WERE HAVING BABIES OUT OF WEDLOCK THAN THOSE WITHIN MARRIAGE. A COMBINATION OF TEEN AGE PREGNANCIES, AND THE DIVORCE RATE ESCALATION HAVE CREATED A GREATER ATMOSPHERE OF FREEDOM FOR THOSE THAT WOULD INVADE OUR HOMES TO TAKE OUR CHILDREN. FOR YEARS WE HAVE KNOWN THAT MOST CRIMES COME FROM SINGLE PARENT HOMES.

WHEN EIGHTY PERCENT OF CRIMES COME FROM SINGLE PARENT HOMES, THERE SHOULD BE A VERY COMPELING EFFORT TO KEEP FAMILIES UNITED. AT ONE TIME IT WAS ALMOST IMPOSSIBLE TO FIND BLACK CHILDREN IN THE OUT OF HOME PLACEMENT SYSTEM BECAUSE OF THE MOVE IN WITH ME AND I WILL RAISE YOU SPIRIT IF YOUR PARENTS DIED OR A TRAGEDY OCCURRED IN A BLACK FAMILY. THIS SPIRIT EXISTED BECAUSE OF THE OPEN HATRED SHOWN AND DISPLAYED IN AMERICA'S SEGRAGATION AND JIM-CROW LAWS

IN THOSE YEARS. THIS SPIRIT HAS CHANGED TODAY. BLACKS FIND THEIR CHILDREN THE HIGHEST RATED TARGETS IN MANY AREAS, ESPECIALLY LARGE CITIES.

WHY? ONE ** THE BLACK MEN FROM THE AGES OF FIFTEEN (15) AND TWENTY NINE (29) ARE STILL THE MOST TARGETED GROUP KILLED BY THE POLICE. TWO ** <u>THE PRACTICE OF THE POLICE ENFORCEMENT OFFICIALS TO ALLOW DRUGS TO BE OPENLY SOLD ON THE STREETS AND IN NEIGHBORHOODS FREQUENTED BY BLACKS</u>. THIS PRACTICE HAS RESULTED IN THOUSANDS OF BLACKS BEING KEPT OUT OF CITY, COUNTY, STATE, AND GOVERNMENT JOBS BECAUSE OF DRUG ASSOCIATION. IT HAS RESULTED IN THE DEATH OF THOUSANDS BY DRUG RELATED GANG WARS. MANY OF THESE WERE DELIBERATLY PROVOKED BY OUTSIDERS.

<u>THREE ** THE LAST HIRED AND FIRST FIRED POLICY OF BUSINESS IS STILL VERY MUCH ALIVE. . THIS HAS MADE ELIGIBLE BLACK MEN SCARCE WITH LESS MONEY TO CARE FOR A FAMILY. THE MAJOR REMEDY WOULD BE FOR THE BLACK MEN TO BECOME BUSINESS MINDED AND START AS MANY MONEY BASED BUSINESS AS THEY CAN</u>. AFTER ALL MCDONALDS HAS A LOT OF NON-ENGLISH SPEAKING FRANCHISES. HOW MANY BLACK ENGLISH SPEAKING MCDONALDS DO WE HAVE? JUST BE QUIET AND EAT YOUR BURGER AND PIES. A FRANCHISE WILL HELP THE CAUSE MORE THAN A GARAGE FILLED WITH A HUNDRED EXOTIC AUTOMOBILES. WHAT ABOUT A COLLECTION OF 200 PAIRS OF SHOES? GREAT IDEA. EXCELLENT PRIZES ON OPENING DAY. THIS WOULD

BRING DOWN THE UNMARRIED BIRTH RATE AMONG BLACK WOMEN HOPEFULLY BELOW FORTY PERCENT.

A FAMILY'S WILL IS ALWAYS ALIVE

BABYLON AT ONE TIME WAS THE CAPITOL SEAT OF THE WORLD. THEY CONSIDERED ISRAEL A THORN IN THEIR SIDE. JERUSALEM WAS CONSIDERED A BAD CITY. TO SOLVE THE PROBLEM, THEY REMOVED THE ISRAELITES AND SCATTERED THEM THROUGH OUT THEIR KINGDOM HOPING THEY WOULD NEVER BE ABLE TO UNITE AGAIN. MANY AMERICAN FAMILIES ARE TODAY BEING SCATTERED BY OUR GOVERNMENT AGENCIES UNDER THE GUISE OF PROTECTION OF OUR CHILDREN. THOUSANDS ARE BEING REMOVED FROM OUR HOMES AND BEING KEPT WE KNOW NOT WHERE. THE PATTERN IS THE SAME. ONLY THE NAME IS DIFFERENT.

THIS TIME IT IS MY CHILDREN AND YOUR CHILDREN. FAMILIES CANNOT AND WILL NOT STAY DOWN. WILL YOUR CHILDREN RISE AGAIN WITH YOUR HOPES, VALUES, GOALS AND DREAMS? OR WILL SOMEONE ELSE PROGRAM YOUR CHILD? IF MY CHILDREN ARE FORCED TO BE PROGRAMED BY ANOTHER PERSON TODAY, THAT SAME PROGRAMER WILL STAND READY TO PROGRAM YOUR CHILD TOMORROW.

JERUSALEM AROSE AGAIN AND AGAIN THE WORLD POWER AT THAT TIME HAD TO DEAL WITH A PEOPLE THAT SAID, WE ARE A FAMILY. WE MAKE UP THE NATION.

THE NEXT WORLD POWER HAD TO DEAL WITH THE SAME SPIRIT. THE FAMILY IS THE NATION. FAMILIES WILL NEVER DIE UNLESS THE PARENTS LET THEM SELVES DIE. EVERY GOVERNMENT MUST DECIDE WHETHER THE PEOPLE RULE THE GOVERNMENT OR WHETHER OR NOT THE GOVERNMENT RULE THE PEOPLE.

OUR GOVERNMENT IS SUPPOSED TO BE BY THE PEOPLE, FOR THE PEOPLE. THE GOVERNMENT OF ROME WAS CENTRAL RULE BY CENTRAL POWER. THE WILL OF THE PEOPLE WAS HONORED AT FIRST BUT TRAMPLED IN LATER YEARS. JERUSALEM WAS A MAJOR PROBLEM BECAUSE OF BOTH THEIR RELIGIOUS BASED AND FAMILY PRACTICES. THE CITY BECAME A TARGET AND AN EXAMPLE TO THE NATIONS. ROME SLAUGHTERED THE RESISTANT WITH A GREAT SLAUGHTER. THE REST OF THE PEOPLE OF JERUSALEM WERE SCATTERED THROUGHOUT THE WORLD. ROME WENT SO FAR AS TO PULL DOWN BUILDINGS AND PLOW PARTS OF THE CITY WITH OXEN. YET JERUSALEM HAS RISEN AGAIN.

THE PATTERN NEVER CHANGES. A POWER GRAB MUST CONTROL THE FAMILIES. THE FAMILY MUST BE EITHER CONDITIONED BY EDUCATION OR CONTROLLED BY FEAR AND INTIMIDATION. THE AMERICAN FAMILY HAS COME TOO FAR TO BE INTIMIDATED BUT WE ARE STILL TOO NAÏVE TO BELIEVE THAT A NATIONAL AGENCY IS RUNNING ROUGHSHOD OVER OUR FAMILIES. A PART OF EVERY PARENT'S JOB IS TO INSTILL THE KNOWLEDGE THAT FEAR IS NEVER TO STOP OR SLOW PERSONAL

FAMILY PROGRESS. THE END OF FAMILY FREEDOM IS FAMILY SERVITUDE OR FAMILY SLAVERY.

IT IS ALWAYS POSSIBLE TO SEE THE END FROM THE BEGINNING IF WE WILL ONLY ALLOW OURSELVES TO ACCEPT IT. CAN YOU SEE WHAT IT IS LIKE TO BE MOVED INTO A STRANGER'S HOUSE UNDER PROTEST? WHO CAN YOU TALK TO? WHO CAN YOU TRUST? CAN YOU HIDE FROM YOUR OVERSEER? TOO OFTEN WE RETREAT INWARDLY. OUR MIND BECOMES A REFUGE AND THE MENTAL ANGUISH ROAD BECOMES OUR PATH. YOUR SPIRIT HAS ALREADY BEEN PROGRAMED BY THE ETERNAL GOD TO PROVIDE THE PEACE NEEDED FOR BOTH PARENT AND CHILD. STILL IT IS THE PARENT'S RESPONSIBILITY TO LEAD OR TAKE THE CHILD THERE. NO SYSTEM CAN REPLACE THE PARENT. A CHILD NEEDS TRUST AND HOPE TO DEVELOP. ONLY A PARENT CAN PROVIDE THE RIGHT FORMULA. HOPE AND TRUST EQUALS PEACE, BOTH MENTALLY AND PHYSICSALLY.

9. <u>CAN I WRITE MY OWN LAW</u>

<u>TO WRITE A LAW TO REUNITE A FAMILY AND TO SEEK AN ADOPTION HOME FOR A CHILD AT THE SAME TIME IS SCIENCE FICTION. ANTI GRAVITY ONLY WORKS NATURALY IN OUTER SPACE. EXERPT FROM TITLE 19-508 OF THE COLORADO CHILDREN'S CODE STATES THAT EFFORTS TO PLACE A CHILD FOR ADOPTION OR WITH A LEGAL GUARDIAN OR CUSTODIAN MAY BE MADE CONCURRENTLY WITH REASONABLE EFFORTS TO PRESERVE AND REUNIFY THE FAMILY. ASK STAR TREK HOW THAT WORKS. IT IS A FORMULA THAT IN TIMES PAST HAS BEEN INTERPRETED AS AN ADOPTION RACKET WITH OUR CHILDREN BECOMING THE GRAND PRIZE. READ THE STATEMENT AGAIN AND SEE IF YOU AGREE. IS THIS A VALID LAW OR A CHARADE?</u>

1200 CHILDREN LOST THEIR PARENTS IN THE AFGHANISTAN AND IRAQ WAR WAS PART OF A GREAT ARTICLE IN THE APRIL 24 ISSUE OF NEWSWEEK IN 2006. IT WAS POINTED OUT THAT IN SOME AREAS, THE PENTAGON HAS BEGUN TO LISTEN TO SOME OF THE VICTEMS COMPLAINTS AND IS ACTUALLY MAKING SOME CHANGES.

THIS ARTICLE BROUGHT A GREAT JOY TO ME PERSONALY BUT ALSO GREAT FEAR AND CONCERN ***** ABOUT ***** OUR THOUSANDS***

12,000 CHILDREN LOST THEIR PARENTS BECAUSE THE HUMAN RESOURCE SERVICE; CHILD PROTECTIVE AGENCY AND OTHER YOUTH TARGETING GROUPS TOOK THEM FROM THEIR HOMES AND REFUSED TO RETURN THEM. ****** WHY DOESN'T OUR POLITICAL LEADERS LISTEN TO THE CRY OF OUR <u>HOME SIDE AMERICAN PARENTS OUTSIDE OF THE MILITARY? THESE PARENTS ARE NOT DEAD. YET HERE IN AMERICA, THEIR CHILDREN ARE BEING WITHHELD FROM THEM AND BEING GIVEN TO OTHERS. SOME OF THESE STORIES ARE FRIGHTENING. ESPECIALLY THOSE THAT HAVE ENDED UP IN THE HANDS OF CULTS.</u>

OUR MEN CARRIED GUNS AND DIED WHILE FIGHTING TO LIBERATE SOMEONE ELSE' CHILDREN IN OTHER COUNTRIES. WHAT HAS HAPPENED TO OUR LEADERSHIP AND OUR NATION? WHEN ARE OTHER NATIONS AND THEIR CHILDREN MORE IMPORTANT THAN OUR OWN NATION AND OUR OWN CHILDREN? ARE OUR MEN AND WOMEN BORN TO LIVE AND DIE FOR OTHER NATIONS AND THEIR FAMILIES AND NOT FOR THEIR OWN PERSONAL CHILDREN AND FAMILIES? IN OUR OWN COUNTRY, OUR AMERICA, OUR PARENTS ARE NOT DEAD BUT WE REFUSE TO LIBERATE THEM TO RAISE THEIR OWN FAMILIES.

CAN WE RECOGNIZE OUR DIRECTION? HAVE WE BEEN DESENSITISED TO OUR OWN HOMES AND OUR OWN NATION WHILE FOCUSING OUR EYES ON THOSE ACROSS THE SEA?

ONE OF THE FIRST QUESTIONS ASKED WHEN A CHILD IS REMOVED FROM A HOME IS DO YOU HAVE A CLOSE RELATIVE THAT IS WILLING TO CARE FOR YOUR CHILD? UPON MOVING INTO A NEW NEIGHBORHOOD THE FIRST THING MY NEIGHBOR ACROSS THE STREET ADVISED ME WAS THAT TWO LITTLE BOYS TWO DOORS AWAY WERE THE GREATEST TERROR ON THE BLOCK. THEY WERE ABOUT NINE AND SEVEN YEARS OLD. AFTER OBSERVING DAMAGED CARS, BROKEN WINDOWS AND DAMAGED LANDSCAPING FOR A FEW WEEKS, I TALKED TO THEIR GUARDIAN. A GRAND MOTHER WITH A DAUGHTER IN PRISON. HER ONLY CONCERN WAS A CHECK EVERY MONTH. HER GRANDCHILDREN LITERALLY RAISED THEMSELVES. WHEN DID THE BOYS CHANGE? WHEN GRANDMOTHER ALLOWED THEM TO LIVE WITH THEIR DAD. I WAS AMAZED AT THE TRANSFORMATION THAT OCCURRED IN JUST TWO WEEKS. THEY DID NOT NEED A BABYSITTER. THEY NEEDED A PARENT. THEY BECAME TWO OF THE MOST MANNERABLE YOUNG BOYS IN THE NEIGHBORHOOD. WHY? A PARENT THAT CARED WAS ON THE SCENE.

DAISY HAD BEEN ASKED THIS SAME QUESTION. DO YOU HAVE A RELATIVE TO CARE FOR YOUR CHILD? SHE HAD TWO CHILDREN AND HAD LOST HER JOB AND AS A RESULT, HER APARTMENT ALSO. AN AUNT THAT SHE WAS VERY FOND OF AND WHO ALSO WAS VERY WILLING TO CARE FOR THE CHILDREN WAS CONTACTED BY THE AGENCY. DAISY WAS QUITE SATISFIED WITH THE CARE AND CONCERN GIVEN BY HER AUNT UNTILL ABOUT NINE MONTHS LATER. DAISY CAME INTO MY OFFICE

TERRIBLY UPSET. HER AUNT WAS GUILTY OF MOLESTING HER CHILD. BOTH DAISY AND THE AGENCY FOUND OUT THAT DAY THAT NO ONE LOVED AND CARED FOR DAISY'S CHILDREN LIKE DAISY. DAISY WAS A MOTHER. DAISY WAS THE PARENT. WHO IS CAPABLE OF LOVING LIKE A PARENT? A RELATIVE IS NOT THE PARENT OF YOUR CHILD. WHAT MOTHER IS SO LOW AND DEBASED AS TO MOLEST HER OWN TWO YEAR OLD CHILD? DAISY'S AUNT DID NOT SEE HER NEICE IN THE SAME LIGHT AS THE MOTHER, DAISY. WHAT WAS THE CHILD PROTECTIVE AGENCY RESPONSE? RETAIN CUSTODY OF THE CHILDREN AND SIMPLY SEND THEM TO ANOTHER HOME. THEY CALLED THE SHOT AND WERE INNOCENT. HAD DAISY CALLED THE SHOT THEY WOULD HAVE TAKEN HER CHILD FROM HER. CONCLUSION. <u>IT WAS ALL RIGHT FOR THE AGENCY TO PLACE THE CHILD IN DANGER AND HARMS WAY.</u> TO THEM IT WAS A SIMPLE MISTAKE. TO YOU IT WOULD BE GIVE ME YOUR CHILD. I AM BETTER THAN YOU A PARENT. <u>ONE-WAY GUILT AND ACCOUNTABILITY MUST BE STOPPED.</u>

10. <u>THE QUESTION THAT HAS NEVER GONE AWAY</u>

MOST OF AMERICA HAS FORGOTTEN THE JONESTOWNMASSACREWHENHUNDREDSOFAMERICANS WERE FORCED TO DRINK A POISEN LACED DRINK AND SEVERAL OTHERS WERE SHOT AS THEY FOLLOWED THE LEADERSHIP OF MR. JONES. I PERSONALLY WAS NEVER ALLOWED TO ENTER HIS TEMPLE IN CALIFORNIA. MYSELF AND OTHER PERSONS WITH ME WERE ALWAYS STOPPED AT THE DOOR AND DENIED ENTRY ON THE WORDS THAT MR. JONES IS NOT HERE TODAY SO YOU WILL HAVE TO ENJOY OUR SERVICES ON ANOTHER DAY WHEN HE IS HERE.

ONE OF OUR CUROSITIES WAS THE SOURCE OF THE MANY YOUTH THAT WERE IN HIS GROUP. I HAD BEEN ADVISED THAT HE WAS NOTED FOR CARING FOR CHILDREN THAT NO ONE ELSE WANTED. WE KNEW A LITTLE OF HIS TEACHING AND WERE INTERESTED IN WHERE THE CHILDREN WERE COMING FROM AND WHO WOULD FUNNEL THE CHILDREN INTO HIS ORGANIZATION. THIS WAS NOT ALL NEGATIVE CUROSITY BUT WAS IN PART CONNECTED TO OUR OWN AMBITIONS TO EXPAND OUR FEEDING AND HOUSING PROGRAM, AND AT THAT TIME A DREAM T0 EXPAND THE CHILD CARE PROGRAM. DURING THOSE DAYS, IF YOU

COULD PAY FOR YOUR CHILD CARE AT OUR CHURCH, YOU DID. IF YOU COULD NOT PAY FOR YOUR CHILD CARE, YOU DID NOT. THIS WAS ON A VOLUNTARY BASIS. WE USED OUR OWN FUNDS TO MAINTAIN A CARE FOR ALL THAT WERE SERVING CHRIST JESUS. WE WERE CONTEMPLATING ESTABLISHING A HOME FOR ORPHANS AND WERE COMPARING OUR EFFORTS WITH THOSE WHO REPORDELY HAD DONE SUCH.

UPON NEWS OF THE TRAGEDY IN GHANA, A DISCUSSION AROSE CONCERNING THE CARE OF SO MANY YOUTH. ONE OF THE EX-MEMBERS STATED; THE SOURCE OF THE FINANCE IS NOT THE QUESTION YOU SHOULD BE ASKING. YOU SHOULD BE ASKING WHERE DID ALL OF THOSE YOUNG PEOPLE COME FROM? MOST OF THE PEOPLE IN THAT DISCUSSION HAD ASSUMED THAT THESE WERE CHILDREN OF THE VICTEMS. MOST OF OUR SYMPHATHY AND CONCERN WAS TOWARD THE KNOWN FAMILIES AND THEIR PERSONAL TRAGEDIES. THIS EX MEMBER DID NOT BELIEVE THAT ALL OF THESE YOUTH CAME FROM ADULT MEMBERS OF THIS GROUP. HE DID NOT TELL US WHERE THOSE CHILDREN CAME FROM BUT HE DID LEAVE US WITH AN UNANSWERED QUESTION. WHERE DID THEY COME FROM? WHO RELEASED THEM TO HIM? WHY SO MANY?

CHILDREN TRAFFICKING IN AMERICA AND AROUND THE WORLD HAS MULTIPLIED TREMONDOUSLY SINCE THOSE DAYS. A CHILD THAT IS PLACED IN AN ADOPTION HOME IS SOMETIMES MONITERED FOR SIX MONTHS OR LESS. WHERE DO THESE CHILDREN END

UP AT AFTER THE MONITERING PERIOD? SOME OF OUR STATES ARE NOTED FOR MULTIPLE WIVES AND UNDER AGE CHILD BRIDES. (PER MY PERSONAL INFORMATION SEARCH, UTAH AND COLORADO WERE THE TWO THAT APPEARED TO BE IN THE FOREFRONT AT THE TIME OF MY SEARCH. THE PRACTICE OF VIOLATING OUR YOUNG GIRLS IS INCREASING THROUGHOUT AMERICA. PER MY INFORMATION, <u>AT THE TIME OF THIS WRITING, THE OUTSIDE SOURCE OF THESE CHILDREN ENTERING INTO THESE GROUPS CAN ONLY BE OFFICIALY TRACKED BY AN AGENCY LIKE THE FBI</u>.

THE QUESTION HAS COME UP OFTEN AS TO <u>WHERE DO MANY OF THESE CHILD BRIDE GIRLS COME FROM?</u> SPECULATION HAS OFTEN CENTERED ON THE HUMAN RESOURCE, SOCIAL WELFARE, AND CHILD PROTECTIVE AGENCIES AND OTHER CHILDREN RELATED AGENCIES THAT REMOVE CHILDREN FROM HOMES. THE ADOPTION AREAS ARE HIGHLY SUSPECT BECAUSE THE CHILDREN ARE NOT MONITERED AFTER THEIR ADOPTION BUT FOR ONLY A SHORT TIME. THEIR RECORDS ARE SEALED FROM THE PUBLIC TO A GREAT DEGREE. THE SPECULATION STORIES SOUND VERY CREDIBLE. AS I WRITE TODAY I HAVE JUST FINISHED TALKING TO A YOUNG MAN THAT HAS SPENT THE LAST TEN YEARS SEARCHING FOR HIS SON.

HE DID FIND HIS DAUGHTER AFTER A COUPLE OF YEARS BUT IS STILL SEARCHING FOR HIS SON. WHY THE SEARCH? MANY OF US HAVE HARD TIMES. WHY SHOULD A CHILD BE TAKEN AWAY AND NEVER RETURNED

BECAUSE HARD TIMES FORCED A HUSBAND AND WIFE TO SLEEP IN A CAR FOR TWO MONTHS? IS TWO MONTHS OF HARD LIVING WORTH LOSING YOUR CHILDREN FOR THE REST OF YOUR LIFE? I CANNOT USE SPECULATION TO ANSWER. THE STORIES WRITEN IN MY BOOKS ARE BASED ON ACTUAL EVENTS. THESE ARE REAL PERSONS, REAL COURT PERSONNEL, REAL CHILDREN,REAL SOCIAL WORKERS AND REAL CIVIL RIGHTS AND HUMAN SERVICE CODES FROM A REAL AMERICA. THE STORIES HAVE BEEN ALTERED SLIGHTLY TO PROTECT THE PRIVACY OF THE INDIVIDUALS. MY EXPERIENCE IN COUNSELING AND OFFERING ADVICE IN THESE SITUATIONS EXTEND OVER THIRTY YEARS.

THE STORIES ARE RANDOM STORIES FROM THESE EXPERIENCES. SOME ARE BABIES AND SOME ARE OVER FIFTY. SOME PARENTS HAVE BEEN SEARCHING FOR THEIR CHILDREN FOR OVER TEN YEARS. SOME OF THESE PEOPLE ARE STILL IN THE CUSTODY OF THE HUMAN SERVICES, ADOPTIVE HOMES, AND COURTS IN MULTIPLE STATES AT THE TIME OF THIS WRITING. <u>MY FAMILY HAS RECEIVED SEVERAL DEATH THREATS AND SEVERAL THREATS OF VIOLENCE AND POSSIBLE DEATH ATTEMPTS SINCE THESE WRITINGS HAVE BEGAN. I HAVE RECEIVED VIOLENT THREATS INCLUDING TWO DEATH THREATS AGAINST FOUR OF MY FIVE MINOR CHILDREN IN THE YEAR 2005 ALONE.</u> I PERSONALLY ATTRIBUTE THIS TO AN EFFORT TO STOP MY CAMPAIGN. I HAVE BEEN TOLD PERSONALLY BY STRANGERS, (TO ME),THAT NO MATTER WHAT I SAY OR DO OR WHAT EFFORTS I MAKE MY OWN CHILDREN WILL BE ADOPTED OUT AND I WILL

NOT BE ABLE TO STOP IT. THERE IS ALWAYS A PRICE TO PAY FOR RESISTING CORRUPTION IN HIGH PLACES.

YET TO DECLARE WAR AGAINST CHILDREN OR TO SEEK TO BLACKMAIL THE PARENT WITH THREATS AGAINST THEIR CHILDREN IS A SIGN OF THE LOWNESS OF THE OPPOSERS OF TRUE FAMILY STABILITY. MORAL VALUES NEVER DECREASE. THEY MAY BE COVERED, HIDDEN, OR PUT ON THE BACK BURNER FOR A WHILE BUT THEY NEVER DIE. AS LONG AS THERE ARE HUMANS THERE WILL BE A FEW THAT WILL STAND AND PUSH FOR GOD GIVEN PRINCIPLES. AS LONG AS I LIVE, I INTEND TO BE A PART OF THE GROUP THAT STANDS AND PUSHES FOR THESE GOD GIVEN PRINCIPLES. <u>IT IS MY HOPE THAT EVERY PARENT SHALL STRIVE TO MAKE THEIR HOME A SOURCE OF GOD GIVEN STANDARDS THAT WILL BRING JOY, PEACE, RIGHTEOUSNESS, HOLINESS, GODLINESS, TRUTH, FAIRNESS, TRUST, HOPE, RESPECT, DIGNITY, HONOR TO OUR HOMES AND OUR NATION</u>.

HONESTY IS NOT HARD TO ACHIEVE. WE ARE BORN EMPTY. WE LEARN DISHONESTY. I HAVE BEEN CALLED A CRAZY LUNATIC INUMERABLE TIMES NOT BECAUSE I WAS CRAZY BUT BECAUSE I BELIEVE WE SHOULD LOVE OUR NEIGHBOR AS OURSELVES. MY DO GOOD TO ALL MEN HAS PLACED A LABEL OF BEING DIFFERENT AND STRANGE OVER MY DOOR. MY PERSONAL INSPIRATION IS THE MAN THAT DID NO SIN, SPOKE NO FOUL WORDS, HEALED ALL THAT CAME TO HIM, AND CALLED HIS BETRAYER, FRIEND. HIS NAME IS JESUS CHRIST, THE SAVIOUR OF ALL MANKIND. HIS NAME HAS BEEN THE

MOST HATED NAME THROUGHOUT ALL HISTORY. STILL NO FLAW FOUND IN MAN HAS EVER BEEN PROVEN IN CHRIST JESUS.

THE GREATEST COMPLAINT AGAINST HIM WAS HE SAYS THAT HE IS RIGHT AND ALL OF OUR OWN SELF-SEEKING PREJUDICES AND ACTIONS AGAINST FELLOW MANKIND IS WRONG. HIS LIFESTYLE CONDEMNED ALL WRONG AND JUSTIFIED ALL RIGHT. ARE WE HUMBLE ENOUGH TO SEE AND BELIEVE THE SAME WAY AS CHRIST THE REDEEMER? IF WE ACCEPT HIM AS OUR PERSONAL SAVIOUR AND FOLLOW HIS PRESCRIPTION FOR SALVATION OF BEING BAPTIZED IN JESUS NAME AND RECEIVING HIS HEAVEN SENT HOLY GHOST, WE WILL JOIN THE RANKS OF THOSE EXPECTED TO LIVE HIS LIFE AND LOVE HIS LOVE AND BE HIS EXAMPLE.

IN MY BOOK AFDC CADILLAC AND CHILD SUPPORT LET MY PEOPLE GO,

I GAVE SOME STATISTICS FOR ONE YEAR. DURING ONE YEAR THERE WERE OVER THREE HUNDRED FIFTY THOUSAND (350,000) FAMILY ABDUCTIONS IN AMERICA WITH OVER FOUR THOUSAND SIX HUNDRED (4,600) NON-FAMILY ABDUCTIONS. THE YEAR ALSO HAD OVER ONE HUNDRED FOURTEEN THOUSAND (114,500) ATTEMPTED ABDUCTIONS. OVER FOUR HUNDRED THIRTY EIGHT THOUSAND (438,000) PEOPLE WERE REPORTED MISSING AND OVER ONE HUNDRED TWENTY

SEVEN THOUSAND (127,000) CHILDREN WERE PUT OUT OF THEIR HOMES BY UNHAPPY PARENTS. OVER TWENTY PERCENT OF THESE EXPERIENCED PYSICAL HARM AND OVER FOURTEEN PERCENT WERE ASSAULTED OR ABUSED. DURING THIS YEAR EVERY FORTY SECONDS A CHILD WAS REPORTED MISSING AND OVER ONE HUNDRED FIFTY (150) CHILDREN WERE MURDERED BY NON-FAMILY ABDUCTORS.

WHY SHOULD OVER 350,000 MOTHERS AND FATHERS HAVE TO TAKE THEIR CHILDREN BACK BY FORCE? WHY DID SOME HAVE TO KIDNAP THEIR OWN CHILDREN? SOME FELT THEIR RIGHTS WERE VIOLATED. SOME THOUGHT THE REMOVAL WAS NOT VALID. SOME SAW THE FEAR AND TERROR ON THEIR CHILDREN'S FACE AND COULD NOT STAND IT. SOME JUST KNEW THEIR RESPONSIBILITY AND STOOD FOR IT, MOST OF THESE PARENTS THAT VIOLATED THE SYSTEM AUTHORITY TO REGAIN THEIR CHILDREN WERE PREPARED TO DIE IF NECESSARY. PRISON WAS NOT CONSIDERED AN ALTERNATIVE. IT WAS ONLY A DELAY UNTIL THEIR NEXT ATTEMPT. IS THIS THE STATEMENTS OF THEIR INTERVIEWS? NO. IT IS THE INBRED NATURE OF EVERY PARENT FROM THE CHICKEN, DUCK, WOLF, LION, AND HUMANS. IT IS THE NATURAL GOD GIVEN INSTINCT TO PROTECT MY CHILD. FEAR AND INTIMIDATION ONLY WORKS FOR A SEASON.

THE 4,600 NON-FAMILY ABDUCTIONS WOULD BE CONSIDERED KIDNAPINGS. THE 114,500 ATTEMPTED ABDUCTIONS WOULD BE CONSIDERED ATTEMPTED

KIDNAPPINGS, THIS IS THE GROUP THAT SHOULD BE DISCIPLINED AND OUR SOCIETY PROTECTED FROM. WHY HAS THE HUMAN WELFARE SOCIETY AND OTHER CHILDREN ORIENTED GROUPS JOINED THE RANKS OF THE KIDNAPERS IN REMOVING AND SCATTRERING OUR CHILDREN? WHAT IS BEING DONE ABOUT THE 438,000 PEOPLE REPORTED MISSING DURING THIS YEAR? THE FOCUS IS NOT ON THE PEOPLE WE CAN'T SEE. THE PEOPLE WE SEE ARE THE ONES GROUPS SEEK TO INTIMIDATE OR CONTROL. THIS SEEMS TO BECOME THEIR POWER GRID. CONTROL OF THE VISIBLE FAMILY FEEDS THE VANITY OF A MAN OR GROUP. IT LIKEWISE STIRS THE ANGER, HATRED, AND REBELLION OF ITS TARGETS.

11. <u>THE LAW</u> *** <u>THE RACKET</u> *** <u>THE PRACTICE</u>

THE CHARGE HAS BEEN BROUGHT UP ON NUMEROUS OCCASIONS THAT THERE IS A VERY LUCRATIVE ADOPTION RACKET BEING CONDUCTED THROUGH AND BY VARIOUS MEMBERS OF SOME OF THESE SERVICES. I PERSONALLY HAVE NOT BEEN ABLE TO VERIFY THIS SO I DO NOT ADDRESS THIS ISSUE WITH A COMPLETELY DOCUMENTED CASE IN THIS AREA AT THIS TIME. THE ONLY PRICE I AM TOTALLY FAMILIAR WITH IS AROUND 1990 WHEN A PRICE OF $10,000 WAS OFFERED FOR A BABY GIRL.

THE CONSTITUTION OF THE UNITED STATES CIVIL RIIGHTS AND FAMILY CODE FOCUS ON THE UNITED FAMILY AND THE EFFORT TO UNITE OR REUNITE IT. THE ADOPTION IDEA FOCUSES ON THE IDEA OF GIVEING YOUR CHILD TO ANOTHER ADULT. MANY STATE AND COUNTY LAWS HAVE BEEN WRITEN TO CIRCUMVENT THE CONSTITUTION. THEY OFTEN STAND UNTIL CHALLENGED AND EVEN THEN THEY ARE OFTEN IGNORED, CAUSING INDIVIDUALS TO CONTINUALLY HAVE TO CHALLENGE THE SAME ISSUES OVER AND OVER IN SOME STATES. A CHILD REMOVED FROM A HOME IS QUITE OFTEN NOT PUT IN A FOSTER CARE HOME WHERE THE GOAL IS TO BE RETURNED TO THEIR FAMILY.

THEY ARE VERY OFTEN PLACED INTO A HOME WHERE THE PERSONS ARE LOOKING FOR A CHILD TO ADOPT. FROM THIS STANDPOINT, PSCHYOLOGLY, THIS PUTS THE CHILD IN A BRAIN WASHING SITUATION. THIS PLACES A CHILD IN A HOME WHERE THEIR FAMILY IS THE ENEMY AND THE FOSTER PARENTS ARE THE GOOD GUYS. ADOPTIVE PARENTAL EFFORTS ARE DESIGNED, NOT TO ENCOURAGE RETURN TO THE FAMILY BUT TO USE PERSUASION TO STAY WITH THEM.

THE SECOND MOST DANGERUS PRACTICE THE CHILD MUST FACE IS THE LAW OF MIND CONTROL FROM THE AGENCY ITSELF. THE LAW GUIDELINE EXCERPT FROM THE (NORTH CAROLINA FAMILY A. S.)STATES THAT IF THE CHILD DOES NOT GO ALONG WITH THE AGENCY PATTERN A PERSON TRAINED IN THOSE ADOPTIVE ISSUES MUST TALK TO THE CHILD. THE AIM IS TO GET THEM TO SAY YES TO THE AGENCY. THIS AMOUNTS TO PROFESSIONAL BRAIN WASHING. THERAPHY IS ONE OF THE NAMES FOR THIS SECOND PHASE OF MIND CONTROL.

THESE TWO ATTACKS AGAINST A CHILD'S MIND IS ONE OF THE MOST EFFECTIVE WEAPONS USED AGAINST A LONE, SEPARATED, FRIGHTENED CHILD. WHILE THESE ARE BEING USED AGAINST THE CHILD, A BARRAGE OF ACCUSATIONS IS BEING HURLED AT THE PARENTS AT THE SAME TIME. THE INNOCENT PARENT WILL FACE MANY CREATIVE CHARGES TO VILIFY THEIR CHARACTER AND ABILITY. EVERY EFFORT WILL BE MADE TO MAKE THE INNOCENT PARENT GUILTY OF SOME TYPE OF ORDER OR CHARGE OF THE COURT. THE CHILD MUST BE PERSUADED TO SAY YES TO THE SYSTEM THROUGH

BRAIN WASHING AND THE PARENT MUST BECOME GUILTY BY ACCUSATION OF THE COURT. WORD MANIPULATION BECOMES A HIGH PRIORITY OF THE COURT AT THIS TIME TOWARD THE PARENT. THE END RESULT MUST BE A REASON TO TERMINATE PARENTAL RIGHTS AND GIVE THE CHILD TO THE WAITING FAMILIES.

PERSUASION IS OFTEN SUCH AS *** YOU NOW HAVE A NEW SET OF FRIENDS YOU DON'T WANT TO LEAVE. IF YOU STAY IN THIS HOME WE WILL SEND YOU TO COLLEGE. YOUR OLD FRIENDS MAY NOT EVEN REMEMBER YOU. YOU GET TO GO TO CAMP EVERY YEAR. WE WILL PUT YOU ON THE SOCCER TEAM NEXT YEAR. THE PROMISES ARE USUALLY PRESENT DAY PROMISES WHICH ARE NEVER ROCK SOLID BUT THEY CAN APPEAL TO A CHILD AT THAT MOMENT. THEY ARE A WALL OF CHANGEABLE LIES EFFECTIVE TO AN UNTRAINED JUVENILE MIND.

IT HAS BEEN SAID THAT GIRLS ARE EXTREMLY HIGH PRIORITIES AND SOME COUNTIES HAVE A REPUTATION THAT LITERALLY NO GIRL IS RETURNED TO THEIR FAMILY IF THEY CAN POSSIBLY BE ADOPTED OUT. NO REPUTATION IS VALID IF IT IS NOT A PROVEN FACT. IF A CHILD OR PARENT IS IN CUSTODY IN SUCH A COUNTY, IT IS IMPERATIVE THAT A CLOSE OBSERVATION IS MADE.

TRAGIC SON ADOPTION

BOYS PLACED IN AN ADOPTION HOME THROUGH A BACK DOOR AGREEMENT CAN ALSO FACE A SERIOUS LINE OF IMMORAL ATTACKS. TED WAS INTRODUCED TO HIS FOSTER PARENT AT AGE ELEVEN. ALL CONTACT WITH HIS FAMILY WAS LOST. HE CONTACTED HIS FAMILY A FEW YEARS LATER AND ADVISED THEM THAT HE WAS STILL ALIVE. HE SAID THAT HE HAD BEEN DRUGED AND USED AS A SEX SLAVE. HE SAID THAT HE WAS NOW AN ADDICT AND HAD CHANGED SO MUCH THAT HE WOULD BE ASHAMED FOR HIS FAMILY TO SEE HIM LIKE HE WAS. THIS WAS ONLY A PHONE CALL. IT WAS SIMPLY STATING THAT I AM ALIVE BUT NOT WELL. I AM STILL YOUR SON BUT ASHAMED TO BE AMONG THE LIVING. I AM A USED AND ABUSED SON BY A SYSTEM THAT HAS MADE ME DESIRE DEATH RATHER THAN LIFE.

WHAT HAS HAPPENED TO OUR NATION AS TO ITS OBLIGATION TO PROTECT OUR YOUTH? OUR YOUTH ARE OUR FUTURE. WHO WILL PROTECT A FAMILY ACROSS THE SEA WHILE THE ENEMY IS CAMPED IN OUR BACK YARD? WHO IS THE ENEMY? DON'T LOOK AT THE NAME. LOOK AT THE DEEDS. THE PARENTS AT ONE OF OUR SCHOOLS OBJECTED TO THE PROPOSED CLASS. THE INSTRUCTIONS GIVEN TO THE TEACHERS WAS TO CHANGE THE NAME AND TEACH THE SAME LESSON. NAME AND PURPOSE IS NOT ALWAYS THE FULL TRUTH. IT WAS STATED THAT IT IS NOT THE NAME. IT IS THE GAME.

A FEW ENCOUNTERD REASONS FOR ADOPTION

THERE ARE ALWAYS THOSE THAT ARE UNABLE TO BIRTH A CHILD. ADOPTION IS A GREAT OPPORTUNITY FOR THESE TO ENJOY THE FAMILY LIFE WHILE AT THE SAME TIME HELPING A PARENTLESS CHILD. I WHOLLY SUPPORT THIS.

RESOUTO BOUGHT A RANCH AND WANTED A COUPLE OF CHILDREN TO LIVEN UP HIS ESTATE. A FORMER PROSTITUTE TURNED HARD WORKING AND HONEST WAS PICKED UP ON A WARRANT THAT WAS OVER 18 MONTHS OLD. HER TWO CHILDREN WERE TAKEN FROM HER AND GIVEN TO RESOUTO. THIS WAS THE FIRST CASE THAT I SAT IN COURT AND WATCHED THE ADOPTION PROCEEDINGS. THE MOTHER WAS UNAWARE THAT HER CHILDREN WERE BEING ADOPTED OUT UNTIL ONE WEEK BEFORE THE DATE.

FELICIA ADOPTED A THREE MONTH OLD BABY GIRL. SHE ADOPTED HER SISTER THAT WAS TEN YEARS OLDER FOR A LIVE IN BABYSITTER.

FELIX AND HIS COMPANION WERE GAY BUT WANTED TWO BOYS TO MAKE A FAMILY.

SHARON DID NOT WANT CHILDREN AT A YOUNG AGE. SHE WANTED TO PURSUE HER CAREER. SHE ADOPTED AFTER AGE FORTY-TWO.

CHELSA ADOPTED SEVERAL CHILDREN IN THE ASSISTED PROGRAM SO SHE COULD AFFORD TO BUY A HOUSE. SHE

DOES OWN A VERY IMPRESSIVE HOUSE IN ONE OF OUR STATE CAPITOLS.

PHIL ADOPTED SEVERAL CHILDREN OVER A PERIOD OF SEVERAL MONTHS. I WAS NOT AWARE OF THE REASON. MAYBE HE JUST WANTED TO TAKE CARE OF ORPHANS. TODAY IN THIS COMPUTER GENERATION, I WOULD LIKE TO THINK THAT ANY SUSPICOUS ACTIVITY WOULD BE REPORTED AND INVESTIGATED. PHIL'S ADOPTIONS WERE SUSPICIOUS.

LESTER WAS ACTUALLY A LADY BUT WANTED CHILDREN SO HER AND HER COMPANION WOULD SEEM A MAN AND WIFE.

BILL AND ANN HAD LOST THEIR ONLY CHILD. ANN WAS HEARTBROKEN. THEY ADOPTED TO HELP HEAL THE PAIN.

KRESS AND CHARLES JUST FELL IN LOVE WITH AN ORPHAN.

MATRESA AND SHEBA WERE BOTH SINGLE WOMEN FROM FOREIGN COUNTRIES. THEY BOTH HAD HOMES AND WANTED TO HELP REFUGEES FROM OVERSEAS.

ADOPTION OF ITSELF IS A GREAT IDEA. **** BUT WHY**** SHOULD A PARENTS HOME BE INVADED, THEIR CHILDREN TAKEN, THEY THEMSELVES BE SILENCED AND THEIR CHILDREN BE GIVEN TO ANOTHER TO SATISFY

A DESIRE TO ADOPT, OR TO SUPPORT AN UNDER THE
TABLE ADOPTION?

PHIL APPLYING REGULARLY TO ADOPT A CHILD
WAS GREAT. BUT AS AN OUTSIDER NOT SEEING THE
FORMER CHILDREN HE ADOPTED STILL IN HIS HOME
WAS A VERY SCARY POSITION TO BE IN AS FAR AS I WAS
CONCERNED.

I COULD NOT IMAGINE THIS HAPPENING TODAY.
HOWEVER, I COULD NOT IMAGINE MOST OF TODAY'S
NEGATIVE THINGS DISCUSSED HAPPENING AS LONG AGO
AS THREE YEARS AGO. IN-DEPTH INTERVIEWS ALONG
WITH CIVIL RIGHTS AND CHILDREN CODES RESEARCH
ARE VERY ENLIGHTENING. WE ARE ABLE TO FIND OUT
WHAT IS LEGAL AND RIGHT AND WHAT IS NOT LEGAL
AND RIGHT. THE QUESTION THAT IS SO CHALLENGING
TO US TODAY IS WHY IS THE LETTER OF THE LAW NOT
FOLLOWED IN THE PROCESS.

DO I HAVE TO HAVE EVIDENCE *** TERROISTS VERSUS
CHILDREN

A GREAT CRY WAS GENERATED BY THE
KNOWLEDGE THAT SUSPECTED TERROISTS WERE BEING
HELD WITHOUT BAIL AND SOME WERE BEING HELD IN
PRISONS IN OTHER COUTRIES. THIS TRUTH HAS CAUSED
RIPPLES AND CONCERNS AROUND THE WORLD. THIS
CRY HAS BEEN FOR OUR SUSPECTED ENEMIES. WHERE IS
THE CRY FOR OUR OWN CHILDREN? WE CRY*** LIBERATE

THOSE THAT WE THINK ARE TRYING TO KILL US. ****
THE NEWSPAPERS, TV, AND RADIO BUILT SPECTACULAR
REPORTS AND PICTURES SETTING FORTH OUR ENEMIES
AS HEROES SUFFERING FOR THEIR PRIVATE CAUSE. WHAT
CAUSE? THE IDEOLOGY TO DESTROY OUR HOMES AND
COUNTRY BECAUSE WE HAVE A DIFFERENT PHILOSOPHY.
WHY HAS THERE BEEN NO GREAT CRY FOR OUR OWN
CHILDREN WHO WANT TO STAY HERE AND BUILD ON
THE FOUNDATION OF OUR PHILOSOPHY? WE RELEASE
CHILDREN INTO THE HANDS OF KNOWN HATE AND
TERRIOST TEACHERS AND REFUSE TO GIVE CHILDREN
BACK TO DECENT AMERICANS THAT ARE SEEKING TO
BUILD OUR COUNTRY AND NOT TEAR IT DOWN OR
DESTROY IT.

WE KNOW THAT THERE IS A MEASURE OF
SUSPICION AND SOME EVIDENCE THAT OUR NATION
HAS BEEN TARGETED FOR VIOLENCE BY SOME OF
THESE BEING HELD. SUSPICION DOES NOT MEAN
GUILT. INVESTIGATION OF ANY SUSPICIOUS ACTIVITY IS
OR SHOULD BE IN ORDER. IT SHOULD BE DONE IN A
HUMANE, TRUTHFUL, JUST AND HONORABLE FASHION.
THIS IS OUR NATION'S REPUTATION.

AN OUT OF HOME CHILD IS VULNERABLE IN
LITERALLY EVERY AREA OF HIS LIFE AT THIS TIME. THEIR
PARENTS ARE NOT SEEKING TO DESTROY OUR NATION
OR OUR PHILOSOPHY. THESE CHILDREN ARE NOT
BEING TAUGHT THAT OUR NATION IS THE GREAT SATAN
AND MUST BE DESTROYED. THEY ARE TAUGHT TO LOVE
AMERICA AND THE VALUES IT STANDS FOR. I QUESTION

OUR NATION THAT WILL REBUILD OVER FIFTEEN THOUSAND (15,000) SCHOOLS IN AFGHANISTAN AND IRAQ AND TURN THEM OVER TO MEN THAT WILL TEACH THEIR CHILDREN THAT AMERICA MUST BE DESTROYED AND THEN PLACE OUR CHILDREN IN CUSTODY THAT ARE TRYING TO BUILD OUR NATION.

A CHILD TAKEN FROM A PARENT CONTRARY TO OUR CONSTITUTION AND CIVIL RIGHTS PROMOTES A SUSPICION ON MY PART OF AN INFECTED SYSTEM AND AN INFILTRATED LEADERSHIP INSIDE A GOVERNMENT BACKED AGENCY. AN ERROR IN JUDGEMENT CAN HAPPEN FROM TIME TO TIME BUT NOT ON A CONTINUAL BASIS. AN AGENCY WATCH FOR SIX MONTHS IS NOT ENOUGH TIME TO OVERSEE A CHILD THAT IS ADOPTED OUT OR TAKEN OUT OF A HOME. A CHILD THAT IS INSIDE FOSTER CARE OR OUT OF HOME CARE AND NOT ALLOWED TO REPORT ANYTHING TO ANYONE BUT THEIR HOLDERS IS A CURSE TO OUR NATION. THEY ARE NOT EVEN ALLOWED TO TALK TO A POLICEMAN, A PRIEST, AND ESPECIALLY THEIR PARENTS. WHY? ONE MAN SAID; ME THINKS SOMETHING STINKS IN DENMARK. I SAY, SOMETHING STINCKS IN AMERICA. EVERY PARENT IS REQUIRED BY AMERICAN LAW TO OVERSEE HIS CHILD UNTIL HE REACHES THE AGE OF EIGHTEEN. IN SOME SITUATIONS THE OVERSEEING AGE STRETCHES TO TWENTY-ONE. THE HUMAN RESOURCES OR ANY OTHER CHILD RELATED GROUP SHOULD BE RESPONSIBLE FOR MONITERING ANY CHILD THEY REMOVE FROM A HOME FOR THE SAME EIGHTEEN YEARS. ALSO BE MADE TO GIVE AN ACCOUNT OF THE CHILD'S PROGRESS WITH APPROPRIATE PENALTIES JUST

<u>LIKE A PARENT WOULD BE HELD ACCOUNTABLE TO OUR SOCIETY.</u>

A CHILD IS LIKE A PRECIOUS VASE. IF THEY ARE DROPPED THEY MAY BE SHATTERED. A CHILD CANNOT BE REPLACED. CAN A FORCED HOME REMOVAL DO BETTER THAN A PARENT THAT IS LOVING, CARING, AND WILLING? IF THE CARE IS NOT GUARANTEED BETTER, WHY EXPERIMENT WITH A LIFE? SAPLINGS ARE EASILY BENT WHEN YOUNG BUT WHEN THE SAPLING BECOMES A TREE, IT IS ALMOST IMPOSSIBLE TO STRAIGHTEN IT OUT. WE NEED ACCOUNTABILITY FROM EVERY AGENCY. NOT ON A LOCAL SCALE WHERE EACH SECTION PROTECTS ITS OWN BUT ON A NATIONAL SCALE WHERE WE ALL FACE THE SAME ACCOUNTABILITY. <u>NATIONALY THE CHILDRENS LAWS ARE THE SAME BUT MANY COUNTIES AND STATES HAVE TOTALLY IGNORED THE LAW WITH COMPLETE COMFORT THAT THEY CANNOT BE TOUCHED BY ANY COURT OR PERSON</u>. STILL MORE SO WE NEED THE PARENT TO BE LEFT ALONE IN RAISING THEIR CHILDREN UNLESS THEY ARE WITHOUT A DOUBT UNFIT.

WHEN DOES OUR CHILDREN'S CODE, OUR CIVIL RIGHTS AFFIRMATION, OR OUR CONSTITUTION SAY ONLY FORTY PERCENT OF THE TIME FOSTER CARE OR OUT OF HOME PLACEMENT HAS TO BE JUSTIFIED? WHAT HAPPENED TO ONE HUNDRED PERCENT RIGHT BEFORE GIVING A PARENT'S CHILD AWAY? WHERE IS THE ACCOUNTABILITY?

12. <u>FOSTER CARE PROSTITUTE RING****LIFE INSIDE A FOSTER CARE PRISON</u>

CLARISA'S STORY IS ONE OF THE WORST THAT I HAVE ENCOUNTERED IN MY OVER THIRTY YEARS OF COUNSEL AND ADVICE IN THESE AREAS OF OUT OF HOME PLACEMENT. <u>I CONSIDER HER CASE THE SECOND WORST CASE THAT I HAVE CONFRONTED SINCE I BEGAN MY COUNSELING.</u> CLARISA IS NOW SEVENTEEN YEARS OLD. IN A COUPLE OF MONTHS, SHE WILL REACH THE AGE OF EIGHTEEN. THE SYSTEM PLAN IS TO HAVE A PERSON READY TO BE TOTALLY INDEPENDENT OF NEED FOR OUTSIDE HELP AT THIS AGE. CLARISSA GOES TO SCHOOL BUT SHE CANNOT READ. SHE NEEDS TO BE SELF-SUSTAINING. SHE HAS BEEN TRAINED FOR NO JOB. IN A FEW SHORT WEEKS, CLARISA WILL FACE A WORLD OF CHALLENGE WITHOUT ARMOUR TO FACE IT. SHE WILL BE A WELFARE RECIPIENT, ANOTHER BURDEN ON SOCIETY. HOW DID SHE GET THERE?

SHE WAS TRAINED BY A STATE HUMAN SOCIAL SERVICE WELFARE SYSTEM. SHE HAS BEEN IN FIVE FOSTER HOMES. SHE HAS BEEN PASSED FROM MAN TO MAN. MEN, WOMEN AND GIRLS HAVE RAPED HER. SHE HAS BEEN GIVEN DRUGS AND ALCOHOL, BEEN FORCED TO SLEEP ON THE FLOOR AND IN AN UNFINISHED ATTIC.

SHE HAS BEEN FORCED INTO PROSTITUTION SEVERAL TIMES, INCLUDING BY HER OWN MOTHER. SHE HAS RUN AWAY SEVERAL TIMES BUT WAS ALWAYS RETURNED TO THE SYSTEM BY AUTHORITIES. SHE HAS SPENT TIME IN THE MENTAL WARDS OVER THE OBJECTIONS OF THE DOCTORS. THE SOCIAL WORKER HAS IGNORED OVER ONE HUNDRED CALLS FROM THE GRANDMOTHER AND HER CONCERNED FAMILY WITHOUT EVER RETURNING THEIR CALLS. DID THIS HAPPEN BECAUSE HER MOTHER WAS AN ILLEGAL MEXICAN IMMIGRANT AND HER FATHER A BLACK AMERICAN? NO. IT HAPPENED BECAUSE THE CHILD PROTECTIVE SERVICES REMOVED A CHILD FROM A SECURE PLACE INTO THEIR SYSTEM.

AFTER FIFTEEN YEARS OF SECURE LIVING, CLARISA HAS BEEN TURNED INTO A THREAT TO HERSELF, A BURDEN TO SOCIETY, AND WHO KNOWS WHAT DISEASE SHE IS CARRYING. WHO DONE IT? A HUMAN SOCIAL SERVICE, CHILD PROTECTIVE SERVICE REMOVAL FOR OUT OF HOME PLACEMENT. HOW LONG DID IT TAKE TO DESTROY A LIFE BECAUSE SHE DISAGREED WITH HER FATHER ONE TIME? ONE TRIP TO A SHELTER AND A SKATEBOARD TRIP THROUGH FIVE HOMES TO END UP EDUCATED IN THE VICES OF THIS LIFE THAT MOST PEOPLE TAKE A LIFETIME TO EXPERIENCE. FROM AGE 15 TO AGE 17 NO PARENT MUST EVER WATCH THIS RIDE AGAIN WITHOUT RECOURSE TO CHANGE IT. <u>WHERE IS THE BRAKES FOR THIS SYSTEM THAT SAYS I AM THE RULER OF YOUR FAMILY AND CHILDREN?</u>

HER FATHER AND HER GRANDMOTHER FROM THE AGE OF TWO YEARS OLD RAISED CLARISA. HER MOTHER WAS AN ILLEGAL MEXICAN IMMIGRANT IN CALIFORNIA. HER MOTHER WAS A TRANSIENT FIELD WORKER AND DABBLED IN DRUGS. SHE MADE THE BEST DECISION AT THE TIME WITH THE APPROVAL OF THE GRANDMOTHER. SHE GAVE CLARISA TO HER DAD AND HER GRANDMOTHER TO RAISE. AT THE AGE OF FIFTEEN CLARISA AND HER FATHER DIAGREED ON SEVERAL TEEN AGE ISSUES. SCHOOL REPORTING SHOULD ALWAYS BE ENCOURAGED IF THERE IS HARMFUL ISSUES BUT ORDINARY TEEN PARENT SITUATIONS, WHICH EVERY PARENT ENCOUNTERS SHOULD NOT BE COUNTED AN EMERGENCY. THE SOCIAL SERVICES WERE NOTIFIED AND CLARISA WAS PICKED UP AND PLACED IN A SHELTER.

THIS WAS THE BEGINNING OF CLARISA'S NIGHTMARE. THE SHELTER HAD SEVERAL TEEN AGE GIRLS IN IT. CLARISA WAS IMMEDIATELY CONFRONTED BY SOME OF THE GIRLS. HER MIXED RACE AND GOOD LOOKS WERE KEY POINTS OF CONTENTION. CLARISA WAS ATTACKED SEVERAL TIMES BY THE GIRLS AND WAS RAPED BY GIRLS BEFORE THE WEEK WAS OUT. SHE RAN AWAY AFTER A WEEK AND WAS REPORTED MISSING. SHE WAS PICKED UP BY THE POLICE AND RETURNED TO THE SHELTER FOR A NIGHT.

HER MOTHER WAS CALLED AND SHE WAS TURNED OVER TO HER MOTHER. HER MOTHER WAS A DRUG ADDICT BUT THERE WAS NO INVESTIGATION OF THE MOTHER. HER DRUG USE AND LIFESTYLE WAS NOT

EVEN CONSIDERED. CLARISA HAD NOT LIVED WITH HER MOTHER FOR THIRTEEN YEARS. THE GRANDMOTHER WAS NEVER CONSULTED EVEN THOUGH SHE HAD RAISED CLARISA WITH HER SON. HER EFFORTS TO BE HEARD WERE TOTALLY IGNORED. HER SON, THE FATHER WAS SHUNNED COMPLETLY.

LIFE WITH THE MOTHER WAS A MOST SERIOUS TRAGEDY. THE FARM HOUSE WAS THE HOUSE THE SOCIAL WORKER WAS SHOWN AS CLARISA'S PLACE OF RESIDENCE. IN TRUTH CLARISA SLEPT IN AN UNFURNISHED ATTIC IN A HOUSE NEAR THE FIELD OF WORK. CLARISA'S MOTHER OCCUPIED HERSELF WITH ATEMPTING TO PERSUADE CLARISA TO HAVE A BABY SO THEY COULD HAVE A REGULAR CHECK COMING IN. THE MOTHER OFFERED CLARISA ALCOHOL AND ENCOURAGED HER TO TRY DRUGS. CLARISA SAMPLED BOTH. THE MOTHER'S EFFORTS BECAME QUITE OFFENSIVE TO ONE OF HER BROTHERS AND HE REPORTED THE SITUATION TO THE SOCIAL WORKER. THEY DID REMOVE CLARISA.

HER NEXT HOME PROVED TO BE ANOTHER DISASTER. THIS WAS A HOME THAT SPOKE NO ENGLISH. CLARISA'S MOTHER WAS MEXICAN BUT CLARISA HAD LIVED WITH HER FATHER WHO SPOKE NO SPANISH. CLARISA SLEPT ON A COUCH IN THE LIVING ROOM. PEOPLE TRAFFIC WAS VERY HEAVY. MUCH OF CLARISA'S CONVERSATION WAS IN MAKESHIFT SIGN LANGUAGE. THERE WAS NO MISUNDERSTANDING OF THE QUESTIONS AND INTENT OF SOME OF THE MEN. CLARISA WAS AFRAID TO GO TO SLEEP AT NIGHT. SHE HAD TO LITERALLY

FIGHT OFF MEN MANY NIGHTS BEFORE GOING TO SLEEP. WHEN SHE DID GO TO SLEEP, SHE WOULD SOMETIMES AWAKE WITH A MAN LYING BESIDE HER. ALCOHOL WAS CONSTANTLLY OFFERED TO HER AND CLARISA BECAME A CASUAL DRINKER. THE SOCIAL WORKER FINALY LISTENED TO HER COMPLAINTS AND MOVED HER AFTER ONE MONTH.

A PHILIPINE LADY OPERATED THE NEXT HOME. THE HOME ITSELF WAS A VERY NICE HOME TO LIVE IN. HOWEVER, THERE WAS NO CONTROL. THE YOUNG GIRLS WERE GIVEN NO DISCIPLINE AT ALL. CURFEW WAS OFTEN VIOLATED WITH NO CONSEQUENCES. EVERY WEEKEND THE OWNER WOULD LEAVE TO SPEND THE WEEKEND WITH HER HUSBAND IN A NEARBY CITY. THIS WAS PARTY TIME AT THE HOME. IT WAS ENOUGH TO LEAVE SEVERAL TEENAGE GIRLS IN A HOME WITHOUT AN OVERSEER FOR THE WEEKEND. HOWEVER, THE MATTER WAS COMPOUNDED. ACROSS THE STREET LIVED A HOUSE FULL OF YOUNG ILLEGAL IMMIGRANTS.

THE GRANDMOTHER WAS SHOCKED BEYOND MEASURE TO RANDOMLY DRIVE BY THE HOUSE AFTER TWELVE O CLOCK AND SEE HER SIXTEEN-YEAR-OLD GRAND DAUGHTER AND ANOTHER GIRL TOO DRUNK TO WALK STRAIGHT IN FRONT OF THEIR FOSTER HOME. PERHAPS THE MOST FIGHTENING TIME WHILE IN THIS HOME WAS BEING CALLED TO PICK UP THE GRAND DAUGHTER AT I; 30 AM IN THE MORNING WHEN THE CURFEW IS AT 11;00 PM. UPON ARRIVING AT THE SCENE OF THE CALL, SHE FOUND HER GRAND DAUGHTER AND

OTHERS SO DRUNK THEY DID NOT EVEN KNOW WHERE THEY WERE. THE GRANDMOTHER MADE NUMEROUS CALLS TO THE SOCIAL WORKER. NONE WERE EVER ANSWERED. WE KNOW THAT THE CALLS WERE RECEIVED BECAUSE CLARISA WAS MOVED AGAIN TO ANOTHER HOME.

HOW CAN THIS HAPPEN IN AN OUT OF HOME PLACEMENT CONTINUALLY WITH NO INTERVENTION OR CONCERN WITHIN A FEDERALLY FUNDED PROGRAM. THIS IS NOT OUTSIDE IN A HOME. THIS IS INSIDE A SYSTEM THAT IS SUPPOSED TO REPLACE THE HOME IN A CORRECTIVE FASHION. THE REPLACEMENT SYSTEM AT TIMES APPEARS TO BE TWENTY TIMES WORSE THAN THE HOME BECAUSE THE SYSTEM IS RUN WITH AN ARROGANT, I AM UNTOUCHABLE ATTITUDE AND I CAN DO WHAT I PLEASE. I AM PROTECTED BECAUSE I AM THE SYSTEM.

THIS OUT OF HOME PLACEMENT WAS A TERRIBLE, SHOCKING DISASTER. DURING THIS TWO YEAR FIASCO BY THE HUMAN SERVICE AND OUT OF HOME PLACEMENT EFFORTS, NOT ONE TIME DID THEY TALK TO THE GRANDMOTHER THAT HAD KEPT THE CHILD IN HER HOME WITH THE FATHER FOR THIRTEEN YEARS. IN ADDITION TO LITERALLY IGNORING THE NUMBER ONE CARETAKER IN CLARISA'S LIFE, ALL OF HER CALLS, HER COMPLAINTS AND HER EFFORTS TO GAIN LEGAL CUSTODY OF CLARISA WERE TOTALLY IGNORED. AS OF TODAY, THE GRANDMOTHER IS STILL NOT BEING HEARD

OR CONSIDERED. SHE HAS BEEN THE TUNED OUT VOICE OF THE PROBLEM.

AGAIN AN ATTEMPT WAS MADE TO USE CLARISA AS A SEX PARTNER AND A SEX OBJECT FOR MALES. CLARISA RAN AWAY AGAIN. A NINETEEN YEAR OLD BOY AT THIS HOME WAS GUILTY OF SOLICITING SEX BY INTIMIDATING THE GIRLS WITH THE THREAT THAT THEY HAD NO OTHER PLACE TO GO. AFTER THIS RUNAWAY, CLARISA WAS PLACED IN A MENTAL INSTITUTION OVER THE OBJECTIONS OF SEVERAL DOCTORS.

<u>CLARISA HAS EXISTED THE LAST TWO YEARS IN A SOCIAL SERVICE PRISON. NO TEEN AGER SHOULD EVER HAVE TO GO THROUGH SUCH A TERRORISING SITUATION AGAIN. A FIFTEEN YEAR OLD PASSED FROM HOUSE TO HOUSE, MAN TO MAN, WOMAN-TO-WOMAN, GIRL-TO-GIRL FOR TWO YEARS. GIVEN DRUGS, ALCOHOL AND USED AS A SEX OBJECT. AT FIFTEEN A CLEAN CUT GIRL. AT SEVENTEEN A USED ABUSED GIRL WITH ALCOHOL, TOBACCO, AND DRUGS IN HER SYSTEM. HOW DID IT HAPPEN? BECAUSE SHE WAS REMOVED FROM A FATHER AND GRAND MOTHER AND GIVEN TO A DRUG USING MOTHER WITHOUT REGARD TO FACTS OR INVESTIGATION. THIS IS A CASE FROM YOUR AMERICAN CITY, YOUR AMERICAN SYSTEM, YOUR CHILD PROTECTIVE AGENCY, YOUR HUMAN RESOURCE FEDERALLY FUNDED PROGRAM. YOUR TAXES PAID FOR THIS ABUSE.</u>

THE WORST CASE OF SEXUAL ABUSE ??? *** ???

THE WORST CASE OF SEXUAL ABUSE IN OUT OF HOME PLACEMENT THAT I CAN EVER RECALL IS THAT OF A YOUNG LADY THAT WAS ABOUT SIXTEEN YEARS OLD. SHE WAS PARTIALLY BLIND AND USED A WHITE CANE TO GET AROUND. SHE WAS SEXUALLY ABUSED REGUARLY. I REPORTED THIS TO THE AUTHORITIES AND THE PROPER HUMAN RESOURCE PERSONS. TO MY SURPRISE THE REMEDY SHE WAS PRESCRIBED WAS TO TAKE MANDATORY BIRTH CONTROL PILLS. SHE WAS NOT REMOVED FROM THE HOME AND THE OPERATORS CONTINUED THE OPERATION.

TO TOP IT ALL OFF, ANOTHER GIRL AROUND THE SAME AGE WAS ALSO BROUGHT INTO MY OFFICE FROM THE SAME HOME WITH THE SAME PROBLEM A FEW WEEKS LATER. WHAT WAS DONE? SHE WAS GIVEN THE SAME REMEDY. MANDATORY BIRTH CONTROL PILLS AND THE SAME SITUATION. HOW WAS THE PROBLEM SOLVED? OUR LADIES FOUND THEM ANOTHER HOME AND WE MOVED THE GIRLS ARBITRARILY. WHY DID THE SYSTEM CLAIM AUTHORITY AND REFUSE TO CORRECT THE SITUATION? PAY CHECKS ESPECIALLY WHEN IT COMES FROM THE TAXPAYERS HAS A BIG ATTRACTION. A PAYCHECK WITHOUT COMPASSION OR PROPER CONCERN FOR YOUR CHILD MEANS THAT YOUR CHILD BECOMES AN OBJECT NOT A PERSON.

I CONSIDER THE THIRD WORST CASE THE WORST BECAUSE THE CARETAKER CHOSE TO COVER IT FOR

SO LONG. A CARETAKER HAD A SON AROUND THE EIGHTEEN-YEAR AGE BRACKET. HE WAS GUILTY OF HAVING SEX WITH THE GIRLS IN THE HOME WITH HIS PARENTS KNOWLEDGE. THE GIRLS IN THE HOME WERE AROUND TWELVE TO FOURTEEN YEARS OLD. IRONICALLY WHEN THE GIRLS REPORTED THIS TO THE SOCIAL WORKER, SHE DID NOT BELIEVE THEM. ACTION WAS ONLY TAKEN WHEN A GIRL THAT HAD TRANSFERRED TO ANOTHER CITY AND ANOTHER HOME REPORTED THIS TO HER NEW SOCIAL WORKER. COULD YOU SLEEP EASY IF YOU DID NOT KNOW THAT YOUR CHILD WAS PROTECTED FROM THIS TYPE OF ACTIVITY IN OUT OF HOME PLACEMENT? DO THESE THINGS HAPPEN IN A HOME OR IN A FOSTER CARE PRISON? WHERE IS THE ACCOUNTABILITY? IF THE SYSTEM IS WRONG OR CORRUPT, WHO OVERSEES IT? WHY IS THERE A FIRM ORDER THAT THEY ARE NOT ALLOWED TO TALK TO ANYONE OUTSIDE OF THE SYSTEM TO REPORT SUSCH CRIMES?

13. __RESISTING OUR FREEDOMS FROM WITHIN THE NATION__

TODAY, THOUSANDS OF OUR CHILDREN ARE IN PRISONS. ARE WE AWARE AS TO THE NATURE OF CAPTIVITY? LISTEN TO THE NATURE THAT YOU CAN RIGHTLY JUDGE THE NAME, OR THE REASON I CALL THEM PRISONS.

I CAN ONLY COME AND GO AT SOMEONE ELSE COMMAND. I EAT AND DRINK WHAT THEY SAY AND WHEN THEY SAY. I EAT SLEEP AND AWAKE AT ANOTHER'S COMMAND. I AM LIKE A PUPPET ON A STRING. IT IS NOT MY VOICE YOU HEAR. ONLY MY TEARS ARE REAL. A FLAG THAT WAVES TO FREEDOM SEEKERS TIES MY HANDS. A CHAIN THAT SAYS YOUR HOME IS FREE SHACKLES MY FEET. MY EYES ARE STRAINING TO LOOK FOR A MOTHER THAT IS FORBIDDEN TO SEE HER CHILD. MY EARS ARE LISTENING FOR JUST A FAINT WHISPER THAT I MIGHT KNOW THAT MY FATHER IS THERE. STILL MY TEARS ARE REAL. THEY COME FROM A HEART THAT IS BROKEN, SAD, LONELY, FORSAKEN BY ITS APPOINTED PROTECTORS, AND FORCIBLY SEPARATED FROM EVERY COMPASSIONATE EAR.

ARE WE BLIND? I HAVE LISTENED TO MANY REPORTS OVER THE YEARS OF CHILDREN BEING TAKEN FROM

HOMES FOR VARIOUS REASONS. HOWEVER, ONE THING HAS ALWAYS BEEN A PUZZLE TO ME. I HAVE NEVER TO DATE HEARD OR SEEN AN ARTICLE COVERING THE INSIDE OF A FOSTER HOME LIFE FROM A RANDOM OUTSIDE SELECTION. DO WE FEAR TRUTH? LIFE CONCERNING OUR OUT OF HOME PLACEMENT CHILDREN LIVING IN AMERICAN CHILDREN'S PRISONS IS FAR FROM A DAILY CELEBRATION. THERE WILL ALWAYS BE A FEW FAMOUS AND A FEW DEDICATED CITIZENS ANXIOUS TO ADOPT THAT ONE OR TWO ABOVE THE GROUND FLOOR LEVEL OF CARE. HOWEVER, DAILY, ROUTINE LIFE IS FAR FROM A CINDERELLA TYPE LIFE. BELIEVE ME. IT IS NOT ALWAYS A GOOD POSITIVE LIFE.

THIS EFFORT IS INTENDED TO SHOW A PICTURE OF THE LIVES WITHIN THE SYSTEM AND THE APPARENT FAILURES OF THE SYSTEM TO OPERATE, <u>AS IT WAS ORIGINALY INTENDED. THE INTENT BEING TO MAINTAIN A UNITED OR REUNITED FAMILY FIRST</u>. MAXIMUM LENGTH FOSTER CARE AND ADOPTION SHOULD BE SECOND AND THIRD ON THE LIST OF PRIORITIES. OCCASIONALLY THE NEWS MEDIA WILL CARRY A STORY WHEN THE MISTREATED PARENTS TAKE UP ARMS AND GO TO THE EFFORT OF SEEKING TO LIBERATE THEIR CHILDREN WITH VIOLENCE. IS THIS WRONG?

WAS IT WRONG FOR A MAN TO SAY AS HE URGED THE FIGHT FOR INDEPENDENDCE AGAINST THE WORLD'S GREATEST POWER *** GIVE ME LIBERTY OR GIVE ME DEATH? HIS STAND BROUGHT LIBERTY. **** WAS IT WRONG FOR A MAN TO SEE HIS SHIP ON FIRE AND

SINKING AND WHEN ASKED TO SURRENDER TO HEAR HIM SAY *** I HAVE JUST BEGAN TO FIGHT? HE WON THE NAVAL BATTLE. *** WAS IT WRONG FOR A BLACK MAN IN A SEGREGATED COUNTRY THAT DID NOT COUNT HIM AS AN EQUAL TO STAND AT A BRIDGE AND SAY TO THE SUPPRESSORS OF AMERICA THAT YOU WILL NOT PASS? *** WAS IT WRONG FOR HIM TO BECOME THE FIRST MAN TO DIE IN THE WAR FOR INDEPENDENCE? THE WAR WAS WON OVER HIS DEAD BODY. **** WAS IT WRONG FOR A MEXICAN WHO WAS STILL CONSIDERED A MEXICAN CITIZEN TO SAY I WILL FIGHT FOR MY AMERICA AND RECEIVE MY FULL CITINZENSHIP PAPERS AFTER I RETURN FROM FIGHTING IN IRAQ? HE WAS PROUD TO STAND FOR A SYMBOL OF FREEDOM, **** THE FIGHT WAS FOR FAMILIES TO LIVE IN A COUNTRY WITH A FAMILY THAT IS FREE FROM TYRANY. MY HOME AND FAMILY CAN BE SAFE. I WANT LIFE, LIBERTY, AND THE PURSUIT OF HAPPINESS. I WANT JUSTICE, EQUALITY, PEACE, AND THE RIGHT TO RAISE MY FAMILY IN MY OWN RELIGIOUS CONVICTION. I WANT TO LIE DOWN KNOWING THAT THE ARMY IS THERE TO PROTECT ME AND NOT THOSE THAT CRY FOR MY ENEMIES. I WANT THE NEWS MEDIA TO MAKE HEROES OF THOSE THAT PROTECT AMERICAN VALUES AND NOT THOSE THAT CRY TO BRING US DOWN.

I AM AGAINST VIOLENCE AND AGREE WITH NONVIOLENT PROTESTS TO ACCOMPLISH FREEDOM FOR THE MASSES. THE WORK OF GANDHI IN INDIA IS A GREAAT EXAMPLE OF ONE MAN THAT MADE A SACARIFICE THAT FREED A NATION AND RESTORED THEIR CIVIL RIGIITS. HE LOST HIS LIFE BUT IT FREED MILLIONS.

ONE MAN AND ONE FREE NATION. ONE LIFE LIFTED THE SHACKLES OF UNTOLD MILLIONS. EVERY TIME A MINORITY IN AMERICA SITS AT A PUBLIC DINING TABLE, OR ENTERS A THEATER, OR EVEN A UNIVERSITY HE CAN REMEMBER MARTIN LUTHER KING JR. WHO GAVE HIS LIFE FOR A LITTLE MORE FREEDOM IN AMERICA. WHY SHOULD SUCH OPPRESSION FREELY REENTER OUR NATION THROUGH THE BACK DOOR OF A FEDERALLY BACKED SYSTEM? OUR FAMILIES MUST BE FREE FROM FAMILY TYRANY.

I WANT A NEWS NETWORK THAT WILL WORK FOR AMERICA AND NOT SPECIAL INTERESTS THAT BUILD OTHER NATIONS AND NOT OUR OWN. I DO NOT WANT MY FAMILY TO BE SOLD OUT. THIS IS SUPPOSED TO BE MY COUNTRY OF GROWTH NOT OF UNCERTAINITY. A MAN OR WOMAN THAT STANDS FOR THE VALUES OF THEIR OWN FAMILY RIGHTS AS GUARANTEED BY THE AMERICAN CONSTITUTION TODAY OFTEN SEEMS TO BE COUNTED AS AN ALIEN FROM OUTER SPACE BY SOME SECTIONS OF OUR SOCIETY. SOME   AREAS OF THE MEDIA SEEM TO PERPETUATE THIS FEELING THAT NATIONALISM IS NOT RIGHT. THIS IS A FREE COUNTRY AND FREE SPEECH IS GREAT. *****I BELIEVE THAT GREATNESS COULD BE MULTILIED IF EVERY PARENT IS ALLOWED TO TEACH AND TRAIN HIS FAMILY WITHOUT UNNECESARY INTERVENTION BY AUTHORITIES.

FREEDOM WAS THE MAJOR PRINCIPLE OF OUR DEMOCRATIC VISION FOR THIS NATION AS IT WAS INTENDED BY OUR FOUNDING FATHERS. OUR LOVE

AND DESIRE FOR FREEDOM HAS BEEN EXALTED AND SPREAD AROUND THE WORLD. WE IN AMERICA ARE HEARLDED AS THE GREATEST CHAMPIONS OF FREEDOM IN THE WHOLE WORLD. THE BLOOD OF OUR SONS AND DAUGHTERS HAS HELPED OPEN THE DOORS OF FREEDOM IN ASIA, AFRICA, EUROPE, SOUTH AMERICA, THE MIDDLE EAST AND IN VIRTUALLY ALMOST EVERY NATION THAT IS FREE TODAY.

WHY HAVE WE CLOSED OUR EYES AND EARS AND BEGAN ALLOWING OUR OWN FAMILIES AND HOMES TO BECOME SLAVES TO A SYSTEM OR IDEOLOGY? WHAT HAS HAPPENED TO OUR IN HOUSE FREEDOM SPIRIT?<u>WHAT HAS HAPPENED TO THE MEMORIES WHEN EVERY DOOR MARKED FREEDOM INSIDE AMERICA OR OUTSIDE AMERICA WAS STAINED BY THE BLOOD OF AN AMERICAN THAT RISKED HIS LIFE FOR THAT FREEDOM?</u>

QUESTIONS *** WHY NO ANSWERS *** WHO CORRECTS

WHERE IS THE CHAMPION FOR FAMILY LAWS TO BE JUSTLY HONORED? WHO STANDS AGAINST A SYSTEM THAT STONE WALLS FAMILY UNITY? WHO LISTENS WHEN INJUSTICE WITHIN THE SYSTEM IS TWENTY TIMES WORSE THAN THAT IN A HOME? <u>WHEN HAS THE CHILD SOCIAL SYSTEM EVER BEEN ADJUSTED FOR RETURNING CHILDREN TO DRUG USING PARENTS WHILE REJECTING DRUG FREE PARENTS? WHY HAS DRUG USE, ALCOHOL, AND SEX BEEN FREELY SEEN AMONG OUR CHILDREN IN OUT OF HOME PRISONS FOR CHILDREN? WHY HAS</u>

RACIAL AND ETHNIC VIOLENCE HELD A CONSTANT PRESENCE IN THESE OUT OF HOME PRISONS?

ONCE A CHILD IS PICKED UP FROM A HOME, WHY ARE SUGGESTIONS, AND LIES USED TO KEEP THEM IN THE SYSTEM? WHY ARE THE CHILDREN INSIDE THE SYSTEM NOT MONITERED UNTIL THEY ARE EIGHTEEN OR TWENTY-ONE WHEN THEY ARE PLACED IN A HOME BY THE SERVICES? WHY CANT A PERSON CHOOSE THEIR OWN LAWYER THAT THEY CAN TRUST RATHER THAN BE FORCED TO ACCEPT A YES PERSON APPOINTED BY A COURT? WHY DO COURT APPOINTED LAWYERS IN THE CHILDREN AND FAMILY COURTS TRADITIONALY APPEAR TO BE THERE FOR SHOW OR WINDOW DRESSING ONLY? WHY CAN A SOCIAL WORKER IGNORE TENS OF COMPLAINTS ON A FAMILY AND NOT BE HELD ACCOUNTABLE? HOW WOULD YOU FEEL IF YOUR CHILD WAS IN A FOSTER CARE PRISON AND YOU WAITED NINE (9) MONTHS BEFORE YOU GOT ONE ANSWER AND ONE YEAR AND SEVEN MONTHS (19MONTHS) BEFORE YOU GOT A SECOND RESPONSE? THIS AFTER WRITING OVER ELEVEN HUNDRED AND FIFTY (1150) LETTERS?
YOU HAVE NO MONEY ** YOU LOSE YOUR CHILD

A LAW OR COURT THAT ALLOWS THE HUMAN SERVICE DEPARTMENT, PROTECTIVE SERVICES, OR ANY OTHER CHILD CONNECTED GROUP   TO REMOVE A CHILD ON ALLEGATIONS ONLY AND SEEK TO BEGIN INVESTIGATING THE REASON A CHILD SHOULD NOT HAVE BEEN RETURNED TO THE INNOCENT PARENT ONE YEAR LATER IS NOT THE AMERICAN CONSTITIUTION. A

YEAR LATER SEARCH WILL ONLY LOOK FOR DIRT NOT FACT.

A REASON WOULD HAVE TO BE FOUND FOR VIOLATING THE WRITTEN LAW. THE WRITTEN LAW STATES THAT A CHILD MUST BE REMOVED FROM A HOME ONLY WITH A PREPONDERANCE OF EVIDENCE. EVIDENCE THAT IS CLEAR AND CONVINCING, PLAIN AND CERTAIN, STRONG AND SATISFACTORY, COGENT AND CONVINCING, SUBSTANTIAL AND CONCLUSIVE, AS HAS BEEN DECLARED IN SEVERAL CASE VICTORIES CONCERNING THIS SAME AREA OF CHILD REMOVAL? CAN THIS SYSTEM BE FIXED? YES??? WILL IT BE FIXED?

ONLY IF OUR LEGISLATORS DECIDE TO ENFORCE THE LAW FOR ALL PEOPLE. THIS INCLUDES OUR ENFORCERS. ONE ARMY GENERAL OUT OF CONTROL CAN BRING DEVASTATION TO MILLIONS OF INNOCENT PEOPLE IF LEFT IN CONTROL FOR A YEAR. OVER 60 PERCENT OF CHILDREN REMOVALS FROM HOMES ARE UNSUBSTANTUATED BY WRITEN LAW IN MANY AREAS. THE PERCENTAGE SHOULD BE ZERO.

WHY IS THERE MORE CONCERN FOR THE RIGHTS, OF A TERRORIST THAN FOR THE RIGHTS, UNITY, AND HARMONY OF OUR CHILDREN? WHY HAS CHILDREN VICTEMS BEEN SILENCED? THE TERROISTS HAVE BEEN TRACKED BY DISSEDENTS TO THEIR CAUSE FOR OVER THREE YEARS AT TIMES. WHY HAVE OUR CHILDREN THAT HAVE BEEN TAKEN FROM OUR HOMES AND DISTRIBUTED ABROAD NOT BEEN TRACKED FOR OVER

<u>ONE YEAR? WHERE ARE THEY? WAS THE REASON THEY WERE TAKEN FROM PARENTS SUBSTANTUATED BY THE WRITEN CODE?</u>

<u>WERE THEY TAKEN FROM THE HOME AND THE PARENT HEARD THE WORDS OF ONE OF THE DIRECTORS OF A HUMAN RESOURCE GROUP IN COLORADO THAT SAID, I KNOW WHAT THE LAW SAYS BUT IT IS NEGOTIABLE. THE SAME OFFICE ASKED A PARENT TO SUBMIT THEIR CONCERNS ABOUT THEIR CHILDREN BEING HELD BY THE COUNTY. WHEN THE PARENT SUBMITTED THE INFORMATION, THE PARENT WAS TOLD; I RECEIVED YOUR PACKET BUT I DID NOT OPEN IT. ****WHY WILL AMERICA TOLERATE ARROGANCE ABOUT ITS OWN FAMILIES AND OUR CHILDREN THAT HAVE BEEN UNJUSTLY REMOVED FROM OUR PARENTS AND OUR HOMES AND ATTEMPT TO SILENCE ARROGANCE FROM IRAN, IRAQ, OR ANY OTHER COUNTRY IN THE WORLD?</u>

YOUR CHILD MUST NEVER AGAIN FACE THE DAY WHEN HE OR SHE CAN BE REMOVED FROM A HOME AND BE GIVEN AWAY AT THE DESCRETION OF A HUMAN SERVICE CHILD CARE PERSON UPON AN ALLEGATION ONLY. AMERICA'S CONSTITUTION STILL DECLARES THAT WE HAVE A RIGHT TO CERTAIN GOD GIVEN UNALIENABLE RIGHTS THAT ALL MEN ARE CREATED EQUAL AND WE HAVE A RIGHT TO RAISE OUR CHILDREN IN OUR OWN HOMES, FREE FROM THE TYRANNY OF ANY CITY, COUNTY, STATE, OR GOVERNMENT AGENCY INTRUSION, EXCEPT TO PROTECT ITS CITIZENS FROM THE DESTRUCTIVE ELEMENTS OF SOCIETY.

A COUNTRY BOY WAS DESCRIBING THE EXPERIENCE OF BUYING A NEW HOME IN THE COUNTRY. THOSE WERE THE DAYS WHEN THERE WAS NO INSIDE PLUMBING AND THE FAMOUS OUTHOUSE WAS KING. THE PRACTICE WAS TO BUILD A MOVEABLE OUTHOUSE ON THE EDGE

OF YOUR PROPERTY. YOU DUG A HOLE AND WHEN IT WAS FULL, YOU FILLED THE HOLE AND DUG ANOTHER ONE FARTHER ALONG THE PROPERTY LINE. YOU MOVED THE OUTHOUSE AND YOUR PLUMBING WAS COMPLETE. HE SAID IF THE OUTHOUSE ON THE PROPERTY THAT YOU BOUGHT WAS IN THE MIDDLE OF THE PROPERTY LINE, IT ONLY TOOK A COUPLE OF SHOVELS OF DIRT TO FIND OUT THAT YOU WERE ON THE WRONG SIDE OF THE OUTHOUSE.

FOR A LONG TIME AMERICA HAS LOOKED UPON OUR COURT SYSTEM AS BEING THE BEST IN THE WORLD. A FANCY OUTHOUSE WITH A DESIGNERS FINISH MAY LOOK GOOD AND ENHANCE THE PROPERTY'S LOOKS, BUT HOW MUCH HEALTHY VALUE DOES IT GIVE THE PROPERTY? WHAT HAS HAPPENED TO THE BEST WHEN IT HAS BEGAN DESTROYING FAMILIES? OUR PARENTS, OUR CHILDREN, OUR NATION, COULD PERISH. THE CHILD PROTECTION ACT WAS GREAT WHEN OUR PRESIDENT SIGNED IT. WHY MUST THIS LAW AND SYSTEM BE USED TO COVER SO MUCH INJUSTICE? FAMILY CRIMINALS AND FAMILY OPPRESSORS MUST NOT BE ALLOWED TO CONTINUE WITHIN THIS OFFICE. OUR CHILDREN ARE AT RISK. OUR NATION IS ON THE LINE.

A LAW IS FANTASTIC IF IT IS USED RIGHTFULLY. IF A CROOK CONTROLS OUR COURT SYSTEM, WE SHOULD HANDLE OUR BACKYARD BEFORE WE HANDLE OUR EASTERN, WESTERN, NORTHERN, OR SOUTHERN BROTHERS. THE SMELL OF THE OUTHOUSE IS TOO DISTRACTING. THE LAWYERS MUST BE THE FIRST TO OBEY SINCE THEY ARE THE FIRST TO KNOW OR STUDY THE LAW. LIKEWISE. THE COURT SYSTEM. HOW CAN A COURT JUSTLY DEFY THE LAW IN THE MATTER OF AMERICA'S FAMILY FOUNDATION? NO COURT CAN BE OR SHOULD BE AN ISLAND UNDER OUR AMERICAN INSTITUTION. ONLY REBELS STAND ALONE. STILL IT TOOK YEARS TO BRING ABOUT THE RIGHT TO VOTE FOR BOTH WOMEN AND CERTAIN CLASSES OF CITIZENS IN AMERICA. EDUCATION IS STILL FIGHTING IN SOME AREAS.

THE FAMILY AREA IS UNIVESRSAL. EVERY HOME IS A FAMILY TREE. NO FAMILY TREE SHOULD BE CUT DOWN UNLESS IT IS A DRASTIC DANGER TO ITSELF OR OTHERS. WHY ARE PARENTS HOMES BEING INVADED AND THEIR CHILDREN REMOVED AT WILL WITHOUT VALID REASON? <u>WHY ARE PRACTICES ALLOWED TO GO ON UNDER HUMAN SERVICE, WELFARE AGENCIES, AND OTHER CHILD RELATED ORGANIZATIONS THAT WOULD REMOVE A CHILD FROM OUR HOME FOR OUR WRONGS OR ERRORS BUT THE AGENCIES ARE UNTOUCHABLE FOR THEIR WRONGS OR ERRORS?</u> WHY? WHY? WHY? ACCOUNTABILITY USED TO BE THE TRADEMARK OF FREEDOM. HAS AGENCY COLUSION AND INSIDE CORRUPTION TAKEN OVER INSIDE WHAT MUST OR

SHOULD BE THE CLEANEST, CLEAREST SECTION OF OUR COURT SYSTEM? THIS SECTION SHOULD BIRTH GIANTS, AND TRAIN HEROES. <u>THIS COURT ABOVE ALL OTHERS SHOULD PROMOTE THE PRINCIPLES OF TRUTH, FAIRNESS, JUSTICE, AND DIRECTION OF OBEDIENCE TO AMERICAN LAWS. OUR CHILDREN ARE FUTURE GIANTS AND HEROES.</u>

14. <u>A CHILD IN PRISON AND A PARENT ON PAROLE</u>

THE WISE MAN SOLOMON ONCE SAID THAT A CHILD LEFT TO HIMSELF WOULD BRING HIS MOTHER TO SHAME. PR. 29; 15 THIS SAME VERSE ALSO ADVOCATES THE VALUE OF DISICIPLINE. FOR A NATION THAT PRIDES ITSELF IN BEING THE WORLD'S GREATEST EXAMPLE, WE HAVE BELITTLED OUR OWN SELVES BY PERMITING OPEN DEFIANCE OF OUR LAWS BY THOSE WHOSE JOB IT IS TO UPHOLD THE LAWS. THIS PRACTICE IN OUR JUSTICE SYSTEM HAS BECOME EXCEPTIONALY GROSS AND DETESTABLE BECAUSE THE WRONGS ARE NORMALY COMMITTED AGAINST THOSE THAT CANNOT PROTECT THEMSELVES. THOUSANDS OF OUR CHILDREN ARE BEING PUT IN CHILDREN'S PRISONS EVERY MONTH WHILE THEIR PARENTS ARE BEING PUT ON PAROLE AND MUST LIVE AS A CRIMINAL. ACCUSED, DENIED, AND BRANDED FOR LIFE. THE CHILD ABUSER LABEL NEVER LEAVES YOU IN OUR JUSTICE SYSTEM AS IT STANDS TODAY.

A PERSON ACCUSED OF EITHER SPOUSAL ABUSE, OR CHILD ABUSE HAS THIS CHARGE ON HIS RECORD FOREVER IN AMERICA. EVEN IF THE CHARGE IS CLEARED, THE FACT THAT THE PERSON WAS ONCE CHARGED, DOES NOT GO AWAY. THIS CHARGE ON A PERSON'S RECORD ALWAYS RAISES A POSSIBLE GUILTY FLAG TO

ANY REVIEWER OF ISSUES, INCIDENTS, AND RESUMES ETC.

THE PAROLEE HAS BEEN SENTENCED TO A COURT ORDERED LIFESTYLE FOR A PERIOD OF TIME. A CHILD THAT HAS BEEN PLACED IN AN OUT OF HOME PRISON HAS A PARENT THAT HAS BEEN SENTENCED BY A COURT TO BECOME SUBJECT TO IT. <u>NO NORMAL, FAITHFUL, LOVING PARENT WILL GLADLY SUBMIT TO AN OUTSIDER DIRECTING HIS LIFESTYLE INSIDE HIS HOME. ONLY A FELON WITH A JUST REASON FOR BEING ON PAROLE CAN BE EXPECTED TO WILLINGLY OR FAITHFULLY COMPLY WITH SUCH A REQUEST.</u> OUR TOTAL SYSTEM IS NOT CORRUPT.

YET LIFE IS LIKE A HIGHWAY THAT YOU DRIVE EVERY DAY TO WORK. YOU NEVER THINK ABOUT IT UNTIL THE DAY YOU HAVE AN ACCIDENT. THAT IS THE DAY YOU REMEMBER THE REST OF YOUR LIFE. A STORY SURFACED ABOUT A PARENT IN ANOTHER COUNTRY. THE MOTHER SOLD HER EIGHT YEAR OLD CHILD FOR A SUBSTANTUAL SUM TO A PERSON ONLY TO FIND OUT LATER THAT THE CHILD WAS BEING USED IN A PROSTITUTION OPERATION. THIS WAS A HORRENDOUS ACT. STILL WHAT COULD BE WORSE WHEN A MOTHER LOSES HER CHILD IN AMERICA FOR NO VALID REASON AND A WAITING ADOPTION PERSON WITH A BACK DOOR CONNECTION AND A FIST FULL OF DOLLARS CAN RECEIVE HIS CUSTOM ORDERED CHILD THAT MAY BELONG TO ONE OF YOU? A CHILD IN A HOME IS A NATION CHANGER.

THEY ARE GOVERNORS, PRESIDENTS, SCIENTISTS, FIREMEN, NURSES, AND CEOS ETC. WHY DO SOME AGENCIES TREAT THEM AS ROTTEN APPLES ON THE GROUND THAT CAN BE DESTROYED WITHOUT A LOSS? <u>A PARENTS POSITION AND RIGHTS MUST BE SUPPORTED AND PROTECTED AS OUR CONSTITUTION INTENDED IF WE IN AMERICA ARE TO SURVIVE. A SOLID HOME WITHOUT GOVERNMENT INTERFERENCE IS SOLID FREEDOM AND THIS IS A SOLID FUTURE</u>

A WOUNDED SPIRIT IS LIKE A COILED SERPENT

EVERY PARENT WITH AN OUT OF HOME CHILD IN THE HANDS OF THE HUMAN SERVICES THAT THEY DEEM UNJUSTIFIED IS A SMOLDERING SAFETY MATCH WITH THE POSSIBILITY OF EXPLODING INTO FLAME. HOW CAN A PERSON THAT HAS LOST A CHILD TO SUCH AN ERROR WITHIN THIS SYSTEM BE EXPECTED TO BE LOYAL IN BOTH WORD AND DEED? EVERY PARENT AND THEIR SIBLINGS CAN POSSIBLY BECOME ANTI-AMERICAN AND ANTI GOVERNMENT IN THE COUNTRY OF THEIR BIRTH<u>. ANY MAN OR WOMAN THAT STANDS IDLY BY AND ALLOWS THEIR CHILDREN TO BE REMOVED FROM THEIR HOME WHILE BEING THEMSELVES INNOCENT OF ANY WRONG DOING IS LESS THAN A PARENT AND EVEN MORE SO LESS THAN THE AMERICAN PATRIOTIC PICTURE THAT AMERICA LIKES TO PORTRAY IN ITS HISTORY BOOKS</u>.

MESA HAD BEEN REMOVED FROM HIS HOME WHEN HE WAS AROUND SIX YEARS OLD. HE HAD SPENT

THREE YEARS IN A FOSTER HOME. HIS EXPERIENCE WAS QUITE UNSATISFACTORY TO THOSE THAT WERE RESPONSIBLE FOR HIS CARE. THE RELATIONSHIP WAS SUCH THAT MESA WAS SENT TO A CALIFORNIA YOUTH CAMP WHEN HE WAS AROUND NINE YEARS OLD. MESA'S UNHAPPINESSS CONTINUED IN THE YOUTH CAMP. FRUSTRATION FINALLY OVERWHELMED HIM AND HE RAN AWAY FROM THE YOUTH AUTHORITY IN HIS TEEN AGE YEARS. MESA WENT THROUGH SEVERAL BOUTS WITH THE LAW BUT EVENTUALLY MADE IT BACK HOME TO HIS MOTHER. MESA BLAMED HIS ESCAPADES WITH THE LAW ON HIS STAY IN THE YOUTH FACILITY. MESA DESCRIBED THE CAMP AS A DORM TYPE SETTING WITH ABOUT A HUNDRED BOYS AND A COUPLE OF MEAN OVERSEERS OR COUNSELORS ON DUTY. THIS WAS MESA'S TRAINING GROUND FOR TOBACCO, ALCOHOL, DRUGS, AND THIEVERY. MESA SAID HE LEARNED TO STEAL A CAR BEFORE HE WAS TEN. DURING THE TIME MESA WAS IN THIS JUVENILE PRISON, HIS MOTHER VISITED HIM ONLY ONCE.

THE BITTERNESS OVER HIS MOTHER'S FORCED SEPARATION AND HER INABILITY TO VISIT HIM HAS MARKED MESA UNTIL THIS DAY. ANGER AND FRUSTRATION STILL FILLS HIS FACE AND VOICE WHEN HE SPEAKS OF THOSE JUVENILE YEARS WHEN HE WAS UNABLE TO ENJOY ANY FAMILY CONTACT. HE IS STILL BITTER ABOUT THE LONELINESS HE KNEW FROM HIS FIRST GRADE YEARS ON. HE REGRETS THAT HE WAS NOT SET ON THE PATH OF SUCCESS AND PROSPERITY THAT HE FELT HIS MOTHER HAD PLANNED FOR HIM. TO MESA,

HIS MOTHER WAS DENIED THE CHANCE TO IMPLANT IN HIM A MEANINGFUL CAREER. HE BLAMES HIS BOUT IN PRISON AND A FELONY RECORD FOR THEFT AND DRUG USE ON THE WELFARE SYSTEM THAT TOOK HIS MOTHER AWAY WHILE HE WAS STILL A SMALL CHILD. HIS MOTHER WAS ON PAROLE.

THE COURT HAD ISSUED HER ORDERS. HER ORDERS WERE *** THAT SHE COULD HAVE NO CONTACT WITH HER CHILD. HE IS A WARD OF THE STATE. *** THE TEARS THAT STAINED MESA'S FACE THEN, NOW STAIN MESA'S HEART TODAY. THE HURT IN MESA'S HEART AS A CHILD IS NOW ANGER, HATRED, AND BITTERNESS TOWARD A SYSTEM THAT SHOULD HAVE UNITED RATHER THAN DIVIDED. THE HUMAN SERVICE, WELFARE SERVICE AND RELATED CHILDREN AGENCIES HAVE DEVELOPED AND TRAINED ANOTHER ENEMY AND SEVERAL RELATED FAMILY MEMBERS. HOW? BY PUTTING A MOTHER ON PAROLE AND DENYING HER CONTACT WITH HER SON.

IN MESA'S HEART, HIS MOTHER WAS HUMILIATED AND DENIED HER RIGHT TO HOLD, COMFORT, DIRECT, AND INSTRUCT HIM. HE HIMSELF WAS TREATED LIKE A JUVENILE CRIMINAL AND SHE WAS LOOKED UPON AS THE MOTHER OF A YOUNG CHILD CRIMINAL. MESA STILL FEELS SOMEWHAT GUILTY FOR THE SHAME OF HIS MOTHER'S POSITION ALTHOUGH HE CANNOT PINPOINT HOW OR WHY. HE HAS NEVER STOPED SEARCHING AND ASKING WHY? THERE SEEMS TO BE A SMALL OBSESSION THAT RISES IN MESA OCCASIONALY. IT SEEMS TO SAY IF I CAN FIND JUST A LITTLE REASON IN ME OF WHY THIS HAPPENED, SOME OF THE GUILT AND SHAME WILL

LEAVE. A FOSTER CARE PRISON AND A CALIFORNIA YOUTH AUTHORITY HAVE SEALED THIS THING IN MESA. IT SEEMS TO BE THERE FOR LIFE

IS THE SYSTEM BROKEN ** FIX IT

I LISTENED TO ONE OF OUR FAMOUS POLITICIANS RECENTLY AS HE SPOKE TO A MEETING OF REPUBLICAN LAWYERS. DURING HIS TALK HE SPOKE OF A SUPREME COURT THAT HAD TAKEN A VOTE. AFTER THE VOTE, ONE OF THE JUDGES FOR WHATEVER REASON WAS PAID SEVERAL HUNDRED THOUSAND DOLLARS. AFTER THE PAYMENT, THE JUDGE CHANGED HIS VOTE. THE GREATNESS OF THIS INCIDENT WAS THAT THE HEAD JUDGE BECAME SO INCENSED AT THE APPARENT CORRUPTION WITHIN THIS COURT THAT HE CHOSE TO ACT. HE RESIGNED FROM HIS POSITION THAT THE GOVERNOR OF THE OPPOSING PARTY COULD APPOINT A MAN THAT WOULD CLEAN UP THE SYSTEM OF THE COURT. HE SACRAFICED HIS POSITION AND THE POSSIBLE IRE AND SCORN FROM HIS OWN POLITICAL PARTY TO FIX THE PROBLEM OF THE STATE HE LIVED IN. THAT STATES HIGH COURT WAS FIXED BECAUSE CORRUPTION WAS SEEN AND THE DESIRE WAS TO STOP IT TODAY, NOT TOMORROW.

FOSTER CARE, ADOPTION CARE, GROUP HOMES, RESIDENTIAL HOMES, ARE NOT AS FREE AS MOMMY AND DADDY'S HOME. BOTH MOMMY AND DADDY CARE FOR AND LOVE YOU BECAUSE YOU ARE THEIRS, NOT BECAUSE THEY GET A CHECK TO KEEP YOU IN THEIR HOME. YOUR

CHILD IS AT RISK IN ANY SYSTEM THAT PUTS A PRICE TAG ON YOUR CHILD OR FAMILY. AS ONE MAN HAS SAID, WE KNOW THE PRICE THAT THE GOVERNMENT WILL PAY. SEND THE CHILD TO THE LOWEST BIDDER AND WE WILL KEEP THE DIFFERENCE. REMEMBER THAT THIS IS OUR BUSINESS. THAT IS THEIR JOB.

YOUR CHILD WITH YOUR LOVE IS YOUR BUSINESS. THIS IS A PARENT'S JOB. IS AN OUT OF HOME PROVIDER BETTER THAN WHAT YOU, THE PARENT CAN PROVIDE? CAN AN OUT OF HOME PROVIDER GIVE YOUR CHILD A GOOD MORNING WITH LOVE OR A GOOD MORNING WITH DUTY? WILL AN OUT OF HOME PROVIDER GIVE YOUR CHILD A PRAYER AND I LOVE YOU, AND DON'T FORGET THE THANK YOU CARD FOR THE TRIP TO THE ZOO, IT WAS SO MUCH FUN? OR WILL THEY GIVE YOUR CHILD A SIMPLE BE CAREFUL TODAY?

NO HUG, NO KISS, JUST A RITUAL THIS IS MY JOB SEND OFF. THERE IS NO SUBSTITUTE FOR A MOTHER OR FATHER'S LOVE. WHY DO WE HAVE A SYSTEM THAT HAS DEVISED A WAY AND METHOD TO SEEK TO KILL THAT PORTION OF FAMILY LOVE THAT CAN NEVER BE REPLACED? LOVE IS KIND, TRUE, MERCIFUL, ALWAYS FORGIVING. PARENTAL LOVE ONLY HAS ONE SOURCE. WITHOUT A PARENT, IT IS NOT THERE.

A CON MAN APPROACHED A RESTAURANT CASHIER IN THE MIDDLE OF A BUSY LUNCH HOUR. AFTER A BRIEF CONVERSATION, HE STATED THAT MAAM YOU DID NOT GIVE ME MY CHANGE. THE CASHIER ANSWERED

HIM ACCORDING TO HIS COMPLAINT. HOWEVER SHE REFUSED TO GIVE HIM HIS REQUESTED MONEY. THE MANAGER WAS CALLED. THE MANAGER SIMPLY SHUT HER REGISTER DOWN AND DID AN INSTANT AUDIT OF HER BUSINESS FOR THE DAY TO SEE IF HER REGISTER WAS SHORT OR OVER. THE MANAGER WAS WISE ENOUGH TO HAVE A BACK UP CASHIER ON HAND. THE CON MAN HAD COUNTED ON THE DISRUPTION OF THE MOMENT AND POSSIBLE SPREAD OF FEAR OF DISTRUST AMONG SOME OF THE PATRONS. INSTEAD HE GOT A DESIRE FOR TRUTH AND INSTANT FAIRNESS.

IF THE ENFORCEMENT ARM OF OUR GOVERNMENT COULD BE AS CONSCIENTIOUS AS SOME OF THE DISCUSSIONS THAT OCCUR WHILE MAKING OUR LAWS, WE WOULD HAVE AN ALMOST PERFECT SYSTEM. HOW CAN WE SAY WE BELIEVE IN OUR COUNTRY OUR FAMILIES, OUR HOMES, AND OUR FREEDOMS WHEN OUR ACTIONS SAY THAT WE ARE BETRAYERS OF OUR TRUSTORS? LET US STOP THE DESTRUCTION OF OUR HOMES AND FAMILIES WHILE OUR CONSTITUTION IS STILL FREE.

LATE ONE NIGHT A COUNTRY BOY HEARD

A NOISE IN THEIR CHICKEN COOP. THEY HAD NO TROUBLE WITH CHICKEN THIEVES AND THEY HAD TWO FIGHTING ROOSTERS IN THE COOP SO HE TURNED OVER AND WENT BACK TO SLEEP. IN THE MORNING, HE FOUND TWO DEAD CHICKENS IN THE COOP. A WEASEL HAD ENTERED THE COOP AND HE WAS TOO LAZY TO INVESTIGATE. HE NOT ONLY LOST TWO EGG LAYING

HENS, HE LOST THE BREAKFAST FOOD AND TWO FUTURE CHICKEN PRODUCERS. DO WE WANT TO LOSE OUR CHICKENS TO A WEASEL THAT WILL ONLY DESTROY LIFE?

A MOTHER WITH A MOTHER'S SPIRIT

WE WERE TALKING TO A MOTHER WHOSE HUSBAND HAD HIT THE ROAD AND LEFT HER WITH TEN CHILDREN. WHAT IS IT LIKE TO RAISE TEN CHILDREN BY YOURSELF? THE HARDEST PART OF LIFE FOR ANY MOTHER IS CARRYING A CHILD FOR NINE MONTHS. RAISING ANY NUMBER OF CHILDREN IS NOT HARD. YOU JUST HAVE TO WANT TO RAISE THEM. WE DON'T HAVE MANY FANCY CLOTHES BUT WE HAVE EACH OTHER. WE HAVE A COUPLE OF CHICKENS OUTSIDE BUT INSIDE WE HAVE A LOT OF HARMONY, SMILES, HOPES AND DREAMS. OUR TV IS OLD BUT WHO NEEDS A TV. WE LAUGH AT EACH OTHER. WE HAVE OUR OWN COMEDY SHOW. IN OUR CASE IT IS COMEDY SHOWS.

WHAT ABOUT FAST FOOD? WE DON'T THINK FAST FOOD BECAUSE WE DON'T HAVE FAST FOOD MONEY. A LOAF OF BREAD AND A POUND OF BOLOGNA IS OUR FAST FOOD. A LITTLE MAYONNAISE MAKES IT GREAT. WE THINK ABOUT THE A'S AND B'S THAT ARE GOING TO GET OUR SCHOLARSHIPS AND MANSIONS.

WE HAVE TWO PLANS. STAY AWAY FROM ALCOHOL, DRUGS, AND MORAL DEPRAVITY IS PLAN ONE. PLAN

TWO IS BE THE BEST YOU CAN IN EVERY WAY YOU CAN BUT NEVER FORGET THAT YOU ARE FAMILY AND WE WILL ALWAYS BE FOR ONE ANOTHER. NOW WHILE YOU ARE DOING ALL OF THIS, REMEMBER THAT NO ONE CAN BE BETTER THAN YOU. IF THEY DID IT, YOU CAN DO IT BETTER.

<u>IT IS NOT HOW MANY RIVERS THERE ARE. IT IS WHICH AREA THEY CHOOSE TO FLOW IN</u>. SO IT IS WITH MY TEN CHILDREN. TEN CHILDREN, TEN RIVERS, TEN DIRECTIONS BRINGING WATER AND LIFE EVERYWHERE THEY FLOW. WE WILL WALK RIGHT AND OUR SUN WILL RISE AND SHINE LIKE EVERYBODY ELSE. WE ARE NOT DIFFERENT JUST MORE. WE HAVE MORE AT THE STARTIING LINE SO WE HAVE A BETTER CHANCE TO WIN. SO WE JUST KEEP ON RACING. WE WILL NOT STOP. THE FINISH LINE WILL DECLARE THE WINNERS AND WE WILL ALWAYS BE AMONG THEM.

HOW VALUABLE ARE OUR CHILDREN TO AMERICA

THE UNITED STATES CONGRESS STATES THAT CHILDREN AND YOUTH ARE INHERENTLY THE MOST VALUABLE RESOURCE OF THE UNITED STATES. THE WELFARE, PROTECTION, HEALTHY DEVELOPMENT AND POSITIVE ROLE OF CHILDREN AND YOUTH IN SOCIETY ARE ESSENTIAL TO THE UNITED STATES. CHILDREN AND YOUTH DESERVE, LOVE RESPECT, AND GUIDANCE, AS WELL AS GOOD HEALTH, SHELTER, FOOD, EDUCATION, PRODUCTIVE EMPLOYMENT OPPORTUNITIES, AND

PREPARATION FOR RESPONSIBLE PARTICIPATION IN COMMUNITY LIFE. CHILDREN AND YOUTH HAVE INCREASING OPPORTUNITIES TO PARTICIPATE IN THE DECISIONS THAT AFFECT THEIR LIVES. THE FAMILY IS THE PRIMARY CAREGIVER AND SOURCE OF SOCIAL LEARNING AND MUST BE SUPPORTED AND STRENGTHENED. (EXCERPTS, NOT WORD FOR WORD).

THESE STATEMENTS AND CONCLUSION WERE MADE WITH THE HOPE AND INTENTION THAT EVERY PARENT DIRECTS THEIR OWN HOME. IT WAS NEVER INTENDED THAT ANY COURT IN THE LAND SHOULD USURP A PARENT'S RIGHTS. IN KING DAVID AND KING SOLOMON'S DAY, IT WAS THE PRACTICE THAT SLAVE, SERVANT, AND KING'S CHILDREN BE RAISED AND TAUGHT TOGETHER UNTIL THE KING'S CHILDREN WERE REMOVED TO BEGIN THEIR ROYAL DUTIES. IN THIS ENVIRONMENT, BOTH THE RICH AND POOR, SLAVE AND MASTER, LEARNED RESPECT, HONOR, SUCCESS, FAILURE, JOY AND SORROW AMONG MOST SEGEMENTS OF THEIR SOCIETY. INTERACTION AMONG THE CLASSES BROUGHT GREATER UNDERSTANDING AND IT WAS INJECTED IN THE YOUTH OF FUTURE LEADERS.

AMERICA'S RICH LEADER CONCEPT HAS ALMOST DESTROYED MUCH INTERACTION AMONG THE RICH AND THE POOR AS FAR AS POLITICIANS ARE CONCERNED UNTIL THE ELECTION CAMPAIGNS BEGIN. SHOW ME A PRESIDENT THAT WALKS AMONG THE POOR AND I WILL SHOW YOU A MAN THAT WILL BUILD A NATION FOR ALL PEOPLE. IN OVER TWENTY YEARS OF VISITING PRISONS,

I FOUND NOT ONE RICH MAN IN JAIL. IN OVER THIRTY YEARS OF COUNSELING AND ADVISING AS TO CHILDREN, I AGAIN FOUND NOT ONE RICH PERSON'S CHILD IN FOSTER CARE, OR OUT OF HOME PLACEMENT. EVERY HOME HAS THE SAME PROBLEMS. ONLY THE POOR DOES NOT HAVE THE MONEY TO PROTECT THEIR CHILD.

THE LAW HAS DECLARED THAT A CHILD IS TO BE REUNITED WITH OR KEPT IN A UNITED FAMILY IF AT ALL POSSIBLE. THE PARENT WITH NO FINANCIAL BANKROLL IS LAUGHED AT, HUMILIATED, SCORNED, AND RELIEVED OF THEIR CHILD. THE POOR FAMILIES IN AMERICA HAVE OFTEN BEEN CHOSEN BY SOME HUMAN SERVICE WORKERS AS A PICK AND CHOOSE GARDEN FOR ADOPTION OR INCARCERATION OF THEIR CHILDREN. UNFORTUNATELY THE BLACK AND MEXICAN OR SHOULD I SAY THE POOR MINORITIES HAVE BEEN THE GARDEN OF CHOICE FOR MANY PICKS.

15. __A LOOK INSIDE A CHILDREN'S PRISON__

TODAY AT THE TIME OF THIS WRITING, AMERICA HAS OVER TWO MILLION FIVE HUNDRED THOUSAND (2,500,000) PEOPLE IN PRISON. THE LAST REPORT GIVEN TO ME STATED THAT OVER EIGHTY FIVE THOUSAND (85,000) NEW JAIL CELLS WERE NEEDED IN AMERICA AT THE TIME I RECEIVED THE REPORT. OVER ONE AND A HALF MILLION (1,500,000) ABORTIONS ARE BEING PERFORMED IN AMERICA EACH YEAR. OVER THREE HUNDRED THOUSAND (300,000) CHILDREN ARE DISAPEARING FROM AMERICAN HOMES EACH YEAR. WE USUALLY ONLY HEAR OF A FEW HIGH PROFILE CASES.

WHEN WE CAN LOOK FORWARD TO OVER FIFTEEN MILLION (15,000,000) CRIMES A YEAR AND OVER ONE HUNDRED THOUSAND (100,000) FORCIBLE RAPES OF OUR WOMEN A YEAR, WE SHOULD ASK OURSELVES, HOW DID WE GET HERE? THESE ARE ONLY A PARTIAL RECORD OF SOME OF AMERICA'S DARK WINDOWS. THIS IS FROM THE ADULT SIDE. NOW TAKE A LOOK WITH ME AT THE CHILDREN'S SIDE. I WAS NOT ABLE TO OBTAIN THE NUMBER OF OUT OF HOME PLACEMENT OR FOSTER HOME INMATES AT THIS TIME. THE FINANCIAL BUDGET SAYS THERE IS A LOT. HERE IS A HANDKERCHIEF. PREPARE TO WEEP.

BRETT WAS ONE OF SEVEN CHILDREN.

THEY WERE IN THE YARD PLAYING WITH A NEIGHBOR ON A SUNNY DAY. MOTHER WAS NOT HOME. SHE HAD GONE SHOPING. FOR SOME UNKNOWN REASON, THE POLICE ARRIVED AND PICKED ALL SEVEN CHILDREN UP. BRETT WAS ABOUT FIVE AT THE TIME. HIS YOUNGEST BROTHER WAS ABOUT TWO. ALL SEVEN CHILDREN WERE TAKEN TO A SHELTER. THEY WERE NEVER RETURNED TO THEIR MOTHER. MOTHER DID NOT DRINK OR SMOKE. SHE WAS AN AVERAGE NEIGHBORHOOD MOTHER ACCORDING TO THE REPORTS. BRETTS MEMORIES STILL RECALL THE LONELINESS, SORROW AND SADNESS OF THOSE DAYS. HE REMEMBERS LYING THERE CRYING AND CALLING FOR HIS MOTHER.

FOUR OF HIS BROTHERS WERE SENT TO OTHER HOMES. HE NEVER SAW THEM AGAIN UNTILL THEY WERE ABOUT FIFTEEN OR SIXTEEN WHEN THEY RAN AWAY FROM THEIR FOSTER HOMES AND FOUND THEIR MOTHER. BRETT HIMSELF HAD RUN AWAY FROM HIS FACILITY AT AROUND FIFTEEN. WHEN HE FOUND HIS MOTHER THE SOCIAL SERVICES NEVER SOUGHT TO RETURN HIM. NOR DID THEY SEEK TO RECLAIM HIS BROTHERS THAT HAD RUN AWAY AND RETURNED HOME. THEY FOUND THEMSELVES IN FOSTER HOME PRISON WITHOUT HAVING COMMITTED A CRIME AND NOT EVEN KNOWING WHY THEY WERE THERE. THEY HAD BEEN SENTENCED WITHOUT A TRIAL

THE CAPTIVES ** THE RUNAWAYS ** THE LEGACY

TODAY IN AMERICA THOUSANDS OF OUR
CILDREN HAVE CULTIVATED A SPIRIT TO REBEL AND
RUN AWAY FROM THEIR HOMES. THERE IS AN EPEDIMIC
OF DISOBEDIENT REBELLIOUS CHILDREN. THESE FIVE
CHILDREN HAD THIS RUNAWAY SPIRIT CULTIVATED IN
THEM THROUGH FOSTER CARE. THEY WERE NOT IN
THEIR OWN HOME. THEY TOOK INSTRUCTIONS FROM
SOMEONE THAT DID NOT LOVE THEM FOR THEMSELVES.
THEY WERE IN A HOME BUT NOT FULLY CONNECTED.
THEY WERE ALWAYS OUTSIDE THE INNER FAMILIES
WHILE MOTHER AND FATHER WERE OUTSIDE THE GATE
ON PAROLE. THE REAL PARENTS WERE BARRED AND
THEIR MASTER WAS A STRANGER. WITHIN THEIR HEART
WAS ALWAYS A DESIRE TO RETURN TO THEIR REAL
HOME, THEIR REAL PARENTS. THEY NEVER FORGOT
THAT AUTHORITIES REMOVED THEM FROM THEIR REAL
FAMILY. THEY OBEYED THEIR FOSTER PARENTS WITH A
SILENT SPIRIT OF REBELLION WHILE SEARCHING AND
WAITING FOR THE RIGHT OPPORTUNITY TO RUN AWAY
AND FIND THEIR REAL FAMILY.

THEY WERE IN THE POSITION OF THE AMERICAN
SLAVES SEARCHING FOR THE UNDERGROUND RAILROAD.
WAITING FOR THE RIGHT TIME TO RUN. THEY KNEW
THEY WERE CAPTIVES. THEY KNEW THAT THE ENTIRE
NATION CONSIDERED THEM SLAVES WITH A NEW NAME.
THEY WERE FOSTER CARE CHILDREN. THEY WERE IN
OUT OF HOME PLACEMENT. THEY SEARCHED ** LOOKED
**WAITED **FOR THE CHANCE TO RUN. THEIR BODIES
WERE IN A HOME BUT THEIR HEART WAS ON THE RUN.

MANY NIGHTS THEY SILENTLY CALLED FOR MOMMY AND DADDY. THEIR CALLS TO THE EMPTY WALLS WAS MOMMY WILL YOU FIND ME. DADDY DO YOU KNOW WHERE I AM? EACH HEART ALWAYS CARRIED THE SILENT TORCH OF FREEDOM BURNING ON THE INSIDE. REPRESSED ANGER AND RESENTMENT HAS KEPT IT BURNING. FAMILY LOVE AND CONNECTION WOULD NOT LET THESE CHILDREN FORGET. HOPE AND FREEDOM WILL ALWAYS BE ALIVE IN THE FAMILY BUT SO WILL THE BITTER ANGER OF FORCED SEPARATION. A WARPED FAMILY TREE BRANCH OF UNNECESSARY HATE HAS JUST BEEN GRAFTED INTO A FAMILY WITH SEVEN CHILDREN. SEVEN FAMILY TREE BRANCHES WILL BEAR FRUIT THAT WILL PRODUCE UNGRATEFUL AND UNFAITHFUL FAMILIES TO THIS FREEDOM LOVING NATION. SEVEN SMALL PINHOLES IN A DIKE OF UNITY THAT MUST PROTECT AMERICA IN A TIME OF CRISIS.

TODAY EACH OF THESE FOUR PARENTS HAS A LEGACY THAT IS THE SAME IN THEIR CHILDREN. THEIR CHILDREN BECAME OPENLY DEFIANT OF THEIR PARENTS AT AN EARLY AGE. THEIR CHILDREN ALL LEFT HOME AT AN EARLY AGE DEFYING PARENTAL CONTROL. THEY RETURNED OFTEN ONLY TO LEAVE AGAIN. OVER AND OVER, THIS PATTERN OF LEAVING AND RETURNING BECAUSE OF REBELLION AGAINST PARENTAL CONTROL WAS SEEN IN THEIR CHILDREN. THIS IS THE SAME MENTAL PATTERN THAT THE PARENTS HAD WHILE IN FOSTER CARE WHILE KNOWING THEIR TRUE PARENTS WERE ALIVE SOMEWHERE ELSE. THIS RUNAWAY SPIRIT BEGAN TO MOVE IN THEM IN FORCED FOSTER CARE.

IT HAS NOW MARKED TWO GENERATIONS OF THIS FAMILY.

A THIRD GENERATION HAS NOW BEGUN TO DEMONSTRATE THIS SAME SPIRIT OF PARENTAL DEFIANCE AND A CONTINUAL PRACTICE OF WALKING AWAY FROM PARENTAL AUTHORITY TEMPORAILY. THE FAMILY CONSIDERS THIS RECURRING SPIRIT IN THEIR FAMILY A BY PRODUCT OF THE DAY THEIR FATHERS AND MOTHERS WERE FORCIBLY REMOVED FROM A MOTHER THAT THEY CONSIDERED JUST. THERE IS A GREAT RESENTMENT IN THIS FAMILY TODAY BUT IT IS AGAINST THE AMERICAN CHILD PROTECTIVE SYSTEM. THEY FEEL THE CHILDREN WERE STOLEN FROM HOME WITHOUT A CAUSE. THEY HAVE NEVER FORGOTTEN THE FOSTER HOME PRISON TREATMENT.

THE MURDERER

SPARKY TODAY IS IN PRISON CONVICTED OF MULTIPLE MURDERS. SOME PER MY INFORMATION THAT EVEN THE AUTHORITIES DO NOT KNOW ABOUT. SPARKY BECAME A MURDERER AT THE AGE OF FIFTEEN. HE WAS SENT TO A FOSTER HOME AROUND FIVE YEARS OF AGE AND ALL CONTACT WITH HIS FAMILY WAS CUT OFF. THE INITIAL FOSTER HOME WAS NOT VERY KIND AND THERE WAS MUCH DISSENSION WHILE SPARKY WAS THERE. SPARKY DEVELOPED A RATHER FIESTY SPIRIT AND WAS SENT TO ANOTHER FOSTER HOME. SPARKY FOUND IT DIFFICULT TO CONCENTRATE ON HIS SCHOOL WORK

AND BEGAN FAILING IN SOME AREAS. HE FOUND IT BETTER IN HIS SPIRIT TO BECOME TRUANT IN THOSE CLASSES RATHER THAN ATTEND.

SPARKY WAS TRANSFERRED TO THE CALIFORNIA YOUTH AUTHORITY. THIS WAS A DORM TYPE SETTING WITH ABOUT A HUNDRED YOUTH. THEY DID ATTEND SCHOOL BUT AS ONE FORMER INMATE STATED YOU HAD TO PULL TEETH TO GET AN ASPIRIN. SCHOOL WAS NOT NECESSARILLY A LEARNING EXPERIENCE BUT RATHER JUST A FORMALITY TO KEEP THE INMATES BUSY. YOU LEARNED IF YOU CHOSE TO. IF NOT YOU ATTENDED THE CLASS WITHOUT PURPOSE. IT WAS JUST TO PASS THE TIME.

THIS WAS A MAJOR MISTAKE FOR SPARKY. INSIDE THIS YOUTH AUTHORITY, SPARKY WAS INTRODUCED TO GANGS, DRUGS AND OTHER ANTI SOCIETY ACTIVITIES. WHILE HERE, SPARKY LEARNED TO VENT HIS ANGER NOT ONLY TOWARD THOSE ABOVE HIM IN INSTRUCTION AND AUTHORITY BUT ALSO IN HIS DAY-TO-DAY WALK. HE LEARNED TO VENT HIS FRUSTATIONS ON HIS PEERS. AT THE AGE OF FIFTEEN, SPARKY WAS SENT TO A STATE PRISON FACILITY. AT THE AGE OF FIFTEEN SPARKY WALKED INTO AN ENVIRONMENT FILLED WITH THEIVES, MURDERERS, ARMED ROBBERS, RAPISTS, AND MANY OTHER VIOLENT TYPE CRIME PERSONS. SPARKY AT THE AGE OF FIFTEEN, LEARNED THAT HE HAD TO FIGHT JUST TO PREVENT THE MEN FROM RAPING HIM. HIS FIESTY SURVIVAL SPIRIT AND HIS WILLINGNESS TO DEFEND HIS

PRINCIPALS MADE HIM A MURDERER AT THE AGE OF FIFTEEN.

WHEN DID THIS PATERN BEGIN? WHEN SPARKY WAS REMOVED FROM HIS MOTHER WITHOUT A VALID REASON. HIS JOURNEY OF VIOLENCE AND DEFIANCE OF AUTHORITY BEGAN WHEN HIS RIGHTS TO BE RAISED BY A LAW ABIDDING MOTHER AND FATHER WERE TAKEN AWAY. UPON HIS RELEASE FROM PRISON HIS CRUSADE CONTINUED. RETRIBUTION OR REVENGE KILLINGS BECAME A PART OF HIS LIFE OUTSIDE THE WALLS. HE WAS EVENTUALLY ARRESTED AND CONVICTED FOR AT LEAST ONE SUCH REVENGE KILLING AND IS NOW IN PRISON. THIS IS A LEGACY THAT STARTED IN A FOSTER HOME PRISON.

SPARKY CONSIDERS HIS MURDER CRIMES AND SUBSUQUENT CONVICTION A RESULT OF AN UNJUST REMOVAL FROM HIS MOTHER'S HOME. HE FEELS THAT HE WAS FORCED TO DEFEND HIS HONOR AND HIS LIFE BECAUSE OF AN UNJUST REMOVAL INTO OUT OF HOME PLACEMENT, THIS IS AMERICA'S CHILDREN'S PRISON SYSTEM. SPARKY SPEAKS TODAY AND DECLARES THAT HE WOULD NEVER HAVE SEEN PRISON AS A MURDERER IF HE HAD NOT BEEN REMOVED FROM HIS MOTHER'S HOME ON THAT SUNNY DAY. HE OFTEN WONDERS WHAT HE WOULD HAVE DONE IF HE HAD KNOWN WHO CALLED THE CHILD PROTECTIVE SERVICES AND THE POLICE. HE THINKS MAYBE HIS REVENGE KILLINGS WOULD HAVE ADDED ONE MORE NOTCH COMPLIMENTS OF THE HOME INVASION PRACTICE. HE DECLARES THAT HE

HAD NO IDEA THAT OUT OF HOME PLACEMENT FOSTER CARE WOULD PUT HIM IN PRISON FOR LIFE.

THE MENTAL CASE

DURING A MAJOR FLU TYPE OUTBREAK, BRETT AND HIS YOUNGEST BROTHER, PATCHES ENDED UP AT THE HOSPITAL AT THE SAME TIME DUE TO AN INFECTION. BRETT RECALLS HOW HE WAS ONLY SIX YEARS OLD AND HIS BROTHER PATCHES, ABOUT TWO AND A HALF. HIS BROTHER WAS AT ONE END OF THE WARD AND HE WAS NEAR THE OTHER END OF THE SAME WARD. THE NURSE WOULD COME AND GET HIM TO HOLD AND COMFORT HIS BROTHER PATCHES WHEN HE WOULD NOT EAT OR COULD NOT SLEEP. OFTEN BRETT SAID THE PAIN AND SADNESS OVERWHELMED HIM AS BOTH HIMSELF AND HIS LITTLE BROTHER HELD EACH OTHER. HIS BROTHER CRYING LOUDLY AND CALLING FOR HIS MOTHER, WHILE HE HIMSELF TRIED HOLDING BACK MAJOR TEARS WHILE TRYING TO CONSOLE HIS BROTHER. PATCHES TODAY IS A YOUNG MAN STILL SUFFERING PERIODS OF DEPRESSION AND SORROW BECAUSE OF THOSE EARLY YEARS. HE STILL TAKES MEDICATION TO OVERCOME THE DEPRESSION FROM THOSE DAYS OF SORROW.

YOU CAN OFTEN FIND PATCHES SITTING IN A DARK CORNER OF HIS ROOM. HE SOMETIMES HAS TO BE ENCOURAGED AND PROMPTED TO EVEN GO OUTSIDE OR TO WALK TO THE CORNER. IT APPEARS AS THOUGH HE IS TRYING TO HIDE FROM THE WORLD ITSELF. AS I

WATCH HIM ON HIS BED SITTING IN THE DARK, I CANNOT HELP BUT TO REMEMBER THAT THIS ALL STARTED WHEN A YOUNG TWO YEAR OLD BOY WAS TAKEN FROM HIS MOTHER. HE NEVER UNDERSTOOD WHY MOTHER WAS NOT THERE FOR HIM ANYMORE. HE NEVER KNEW WHAT HAPPENED TO THE ARMS THAT HELD HIM OR THE BREAST THAT HE LEANED ON. A FOSTER CARE PRISON HAD EMBRACED A BABY BOY. A SPIRIT OF LONELINESS THAT BEGAN IN A FOSTER CARE CAPTIVE FACILITY IS STILL IN THE YOUNG MAN TODAY. TODAY HE LIVES IN ONE OF OUR CHURCH OWNED FACILITIES. HIS SELF CONFIDENCE AND SELF ESTEEM IS CHALLENGED DAILY. HE FINDS IT DIFFICULT TO EITHER OBTAIN OR TO HOLD A JOB. SURVIVAL FOR PATCHES WITHOUT WELFARE IS ALMOST NON-EXISTANT. THE BODY IS THERE BUT MOTHER'S LOVE AS A BABY HAS PASSED. IT WILL NEVER RETURN.PATCHES WILL CARRY THIS WOUND FROM FOSTER PRISON FOR THE REST OF HIS LIFE.

MOTHER WAS AVAILABLE BUT HUMAN SERVICE SAID SHE COULDN'T BE YOUR MOTHER TODAY. WE CAN DO IT BETTER. IT CAN BE SAID THAT AT LEAST ONE MORE MENTAL PATIENT HAS JOINED OUR SOCIETY BECAUSE OF REMOVING A CHILD FROM A HOME AND PUTTING THE PARENT ON PAROLE. WILL YOU ASK YOURSELF WHICH IS BETTER? A REAL PARENT WITH A WHOLE SON OR A FOSTER PARENT WITH A LIABILITY FOR LIFE?

'FOSTER CARE CONCUBINE

OF THE SEVEN CHILDREN REMOVED FROM THE HOME THAT DAY, SEANNA WAS THE ONLY GIRL. SHE WAS SENT TO WHAT APPEARED TO BE A VERY RESPECTABLE AND CAPABLE FAMILY. SEANNA LEARNED WHAT MANY GIRLS AND ALSO MANY BOYS EVENTUALLY LEARN. THAT THERE STAY IN A HOME HAS MORE THAN ONE PRICE. IT IS NOT ONLY THE PAYCHECK FROM THE STATE. SHE LEARNED THAT HER CHORES WERE MORE THAN WASHING DISHES AND KEEPING HER ROOM NEAT. SHE WAS A CHILD IN A STRANGE HOME.

THERE WAS NO ONE SHE COULD TURN TO. THE SOCIAL WORKER PUT HER THERE. SHE WAS NOT HER FRIEND. WHAT WOULD HAPPEN IF SHE BECAME UPSET AT HER? THE SCHOOL TEACHER MIGHT NOT UNDERSTAND HER COMPLAINTS OR PROBLEMS AND BESIDES SHE SEEMED SO DISTANT. SHE HAD NO SISTER, BROTHER, MOTHER, OR FATHER. SHE WAS ALONE. THE THREATS WERE REAL. HER PILLOW WAS FILLED WITH TEARS MANY NIGHTS BUT EVEN THOSE HAD TO BE HIDEN FROM HER KEEPERS. SHE HAD HEARD THE INITIAL THREATS IF SHE TALKED. WHAT WOULD HAPPEN IF THEY KNEW HOW BAD SHE HATED THE SHAME, THE HUMILIATION, AND THE GUILT SHE FELT EVERY TIME SHE FELT THE MAN COME INTO HER ROOM? SEANNA WAS USED AS A SEX SLAVE.

IN HER MIND, SEANNA NEVER FORGOT THE CITY SHE CAME FROM AND THE FAMILY THAT WAS THERE.

SHE SAVED EVERY DIME AND DOLLAR THAT SHE GOT A HOLD OF. HER LITTLE GLASS BOTTLE BURIED IN THE GROUND WITH THE TOP COVERED WITH DIRT BECAME HER FREEDOM BUCKET. SHE WAS GOING TO GO TO THAT CITY AND FIND HER FAMILY. SEANNA FINALLY MADE IT HOME. BUT SEANNA CAME HOME A DIFFERENT CHILD. SEANNA WAS NOW A TEENAGER. INSIDE OF HER WAS A HATRED FOR A MAN THAT HAD ABUSED HER. SHE WAS TOO ASHAMED AND FEARFUL TO DECLARE HIS ABUSE BUT SHE HERSELF BECAME AN ABUSER OF MEN.

HOW? SHE SOUGHT TO DUPE THEM OUT OF THEIR MONEY ANY WAY SHE COULD. SHE DID NOT DRINK BUT YOU FOUND HAR AROUND THE TAVERNS OFTEN GLEANING THE MEN'S RICHES. THIS WAS A SPIRIT THAT WAS STARTED IN A LITTLE GIRL THAT WAS REMOVED FROM A HOME BECAUSE A MOTHER WENT SHOPING AND LEFT SEVEN CHILDREN AT HOME. A FOSTER HOME TO SEANNA WAS AN INTRODUCTION TO CHILD SEX IN THE MIDST OF THREATS, FEAR AND SHAME. SEANNA NEVER CLAIMED TO BE A PROSTITUTE, ONLY A COLLECTER OF MEN'S MONEY. WITHOUT VOICING AN OPEN THREAT, HER SPIRIT WITHIN HER HAD BEGAN TO STATE OVER AND OVER, I WILL GET EVEN WITH THE MEN THAT ABUSED ME.

HAPPY MARRIAGE **** IMPOSSIBLE

WHAT ABOUT HER PERSONAL LIFE? HOW CAN A WOMAN TREAT A MAN RIGHT EVEN IF IT IS HER

HUSBAND IF THERE IS A BASIC HATRED OF A MAN IN HER HEART? THE MOST INTIMATE TIMES OF THE MARRIAGE OFTEN BROUGHT MEMORIES THAT MADE CLOSENESS NEXT TO IMPOSSIBLE. THESE INTIMATE TIMES OFTEN WERE INTERRUPTED BY VISIONS OF HER FOSTER PARENT MOLESTER ENTERING INTO HER ROOM. HER BODY WOULD AUTOMATICALLY REBEL AGAINST ANY ATTENTION FROM HER HUSBAND. A SPIRIT OF DISGUST, COLDNESS AND FEAR WOULD MAKE HER SHUDDER. THIS BASIC UNDERLYING FEAR SEALED IN CHILDHOOD MEMORIES HAS MADE A HAPPY MARRIED LIFE ALMOST IMPOSSIBLE FOR SEANNA AND HER HUSBAND.

WHEN DID THIS BEGIN? WHEN A YOUNG GIRL WAS TAKEN FROM HER HOME BY THE HUMAN SERVICES FOR CHILDREN AND FAMILIES ALONG WITH THE CHILD PROTECTIVE SERVICES AND OTHER FAMILY RELATED AGENCIES. AT LEAST TWO GENERATIONS OF A FAMILY HAVE BEEN WOUNDED AND ONLY HEAVEN KNOWS FOR SURE HOW MUCH DAMAGE HAS BEEN DONE THROUGH THE LIVES OF EACH PERSON TOUCHED BY THESE EVENTS

THINKING OF SEANNA REMINDS ME OF TWO CASES THAT HAVE COME ACROSS MY DESK IN THE PAST. ONE CALL PRIOR TO A FIFTH MARRIAGE STATED, PASTOR I HAVE BEEN MARRIED FOUR TIMES AND THIS WOULD BE MY FIFTH TIME. I DON'T KNOW WHETHER I AM MARRIED OR NOT. BUT I CANT LIVE WITHOUT A HUSBAND. PRAY FOR ME. WHERE DID HER REBELLION WITHIN A MARRIAGE COME FROM? WHAT WAS THE

INCIDENT THAT MADE IT IMPOSSIBLE FOR THIS GIRL THAT WE CALL MARY TO HAVE A HAPPY MARRIAGE? ALMOST EVERY YOUNG LADY HAS THE ASPIRATIONS TO HAVE A GOOD MARRIAGE AND A LOVING HOME BESIDE A LOVING HUSBAND. AT WHAT POINT IN HER LIFE DID MARY'S DREAM BECOME SHATTERED? DID IT HAPPEN WHEN HER PARENTS WERE GOING THROUGH A DIVORCE AND SHE SPENT FIVE MONTHS WITH AN AUNT THAT HAD GONE THROUGH A DIVORCE NINE MONTHS EARLIER? OR WAS IT THAT EARLY MORNING SCHOOL REMOVAL AS A CHILD?

ANOTHER YOUNG MAN DECLARED AS HE PREPARED TO MARRY HIS FIFTH WIFE; THIS IS NUMBER FIVE. IF IT DOESN'T WORK, I WILL GET ANOTHER ONE. A LITTLE OVER A YEAR LATER, HE WAS IN THE PROCESS OF MARRYING WIFE NUMBER SIX. I WAS NOT ABLE AT THE TIME TO ADMINISTER COUNSELING TO THIS YOUNG MAN BUT THE AMERICAN PATTERN OF MARRIAGE AND DIVORCE IS ONE OF THE WORST IN THE WORLD. WE CANNOT ALWAYS FIND A REASON. WHILE CHILDREN ARE LOOKING FORWARD TO BECOMING MEN AND WOMEN, LIFE IS WAITING WITH ALL ITS PITFALLS.

A PARENT HAS A PLAN. HOME INTERVENTION HAS AN INTRUSION. A SOLID UNITED HOME AMONG PARENTS IS ONE OF THE BEST GIFTS THAT A CHILD CAN HAVE. THERE IS USUALLY NO GREATER EXAMPLE THAN THE TRIUMPHANT FAMILY OF GOD THROUGH THE FAITH OF JESUS CHRIST. AND THAT IS A CHALLENGE.!!! THERE IS NO GREATER GLUE THAN JESUS CHRIST AND NO BETTER

BANDAID THAN HIS LOVE AND GRACE. NO MATTER HOW THE JOURNEY BEGAN, THOSE WHO FOUND JESUS CHRIST FOUND PEACE IN SPITE OF THEIR STRUGGLES.

STILL, SEANNA'S PROBLEM IS EASY TO PINPOINT. HER ROAD BEGAN IN A FOSTER CARE HOME THAT TO HER WAS A FOSTER CARE PRISON. HER QUESTIONS AT THAT TIME WERE, WHERE ARE MY BROTHERS? I DON'T SEE MY MOTHER. I NEED SOME COMFORT. WHERE IS IT? I HEAR ABOUT LOVE BUT NO ONE SHOWS ME WHAT I CALL LOVE. DOES ANYONE CARE? WHY AM I ALONE IN THE MIDST OF THIS FAMILY? AM I SO BAD? WHAT DID I DO TO HAVE TO SUFFER THIS ABUSE? HER FOSTER HOME WAS A PRISON THAT KEPT HER AS A SEX SLAVE FOR HER FOSTER PARENT.

IN HER MIND, THE SOCIAL WORKER WAS DEEMED HER ENEMY AND COULD NOT BE TRUSTED. AFTER ALL, THIS IS THE PERSON AND SYSTEM THAT PUT ME HERE. THE SCHOOL TEACHERS WERE SEEN BY SEANNA AS PART OF THE SYSTEM THAT PUT HER THERE. HER ONLY HOPE IN HER MIND WAS TO GET BACK TO HER PARENTS. THIS SHE DID AFTER SEVERAL YEARS IN A FOSTER CARE PRISON. SHE MADE IT BACK HOME BUT IT WAS TOO LATE. HER LIFE WAS A WRECK AND UNLESS GOD ALMIGHTY TAKES OUT THE HATRED, THE BITTERNESS, THE GUILT AND SHAME, SHE WILL NEVER REGAIN ANY LASTING HAPPINESS IN THIS LIFE.

A LITTLE GIRL UNABLE TO GROW UP AS A CHILD. NOW A GROWN WOMAN THAT HAS AGED BEFORE HER

TIME. A WOMAN THAT NOW CARRIES THE WRINKLES, NOT OF AGE, BUT OF SORROW, PAIN, ANGER, REJECTION, AND THE LONELINESS OF BEING SEPARATED FROM HER FAMILY. IMAGINE HER FACE AS SHE STATES; I COVERED MY FACE IN THE PILLOW THAT MY CRIES WOULD NOT BE HEARD AND MY TEARS NOT SEEN. I STRETCHED OUT MY HANDS FOR HELP BUT I ONLY GRASPED AIR. FOSTER CARE TO ME WAS A LIVING GRAVE.

16. **PRISON RULES OR   FOSTER CARE**

THE HUMAN RESOURCE PERSONNEL NORMALLY REFER TO OUT OF HOME PLACEMENT AS BEING NECESSARY FOR THE SAFETY AND WELL BEING OF A CHILD. MAN'S NATURE IS NATURALLY REBELLIOUS OR FEARFUL TO ANY STRANGER THAT SEEKS TO EXERCISE AUTHORITY OVER US. THIS IS A BUILT IN SAFETY FACTOR THAT THE ETERNAL GOD HAS PLACED IN EVERY MAN. A PARENT THAT IS AWARE OF THE MANY CHILD ABDUCTIONS, ABUSES, AND VARIOUS CRIMES AGAINST CHILDREN HAVE NORMALLY CULTIVATED SOME OF THESE CHARACTHERISTICS WITHIN OUR CHILDREN. A CHILD TRAINED OR RAISED BY A KNOWLEDGEABLE PARENT CAN BE QUITE A HANDFUL WHEN CONFRONTED BY A PERSON THEY EITHER THINK OR KNOW IS WRONG.

WITH OVER SIXTY PERCENT OF CHILDREN REMOVED FROM HOMES BEING UNJUSTIFIED, THE SYSTEM HAS BECOME A DICTATORSHIP MODELED ON THE ORDER OF THE PRISON SYSTEM. THE RESULT IS NOT A SYSTEM THAT SUBSTITUTES GOOD HOMES FOR BAD HOMES BUT RATHER A SYSTEM THAT SUBSTITUTES ORDERS FOR INSTRUCTIONS, RULES FOR GUIDELINES, DISCIPLINE FOR CORRECTION, REWARDS FOR LOVE, AND A YOUNG PRISON TRAINEE FOR AN OLDER ADULT PRISON TRAINEE.

A MAN IN PRISON HAS A RELEASE DATE. WHEN DO YOU RELEASE A CHILD INMATE? SOME YOUTH ARE SUPPOSED TO BEGAN A TRAINING PROCESS AROUND THE AGE OF SIXTEEN. BY THE TIME THEY ARE EIGHTEEN, THEY ARE SUPPOSED TO BE ABLE TO GO IT ON THEIR OWN. IN SPECIAL CIRCUMSTANCES, THEY CAN BE MAINTAINED UNTILL THEY ARE TWENTY-ONE. THIS IS THE NORMAL STANDARD ACROSS AMERICA. DOES IT WORK? STATISTICALLY? NO. THIS IS THE MOST CRITICAL TIME FOR ANY YOUTH. <u>THIS IS TRANSITION TIME FROM YOUTH TO YOUNG ADULT. A FOUNDATION SHOULD BE THERE OF HOPE FOR LIFE DESTINY. PERSONAL FAMILY DREAMS OF MARRIAGE, CHILDREN, HOMES, COLLEGE AND CAREERS SHOULD HAVE ALREADY BEEN STIMULATED IN THESE YOUNG PEOPLE. HAS IT BEEN DONE IN FOSTER CARE OR OUT OF HOME PLACEMENT? TRADITIONALLY IT HAS NOT BEEN ACCOMPLISHED</u>.

WE PREDOMINATELY GAIN MISFITS AND NOT A FAMILY ORIENTATED SOCIETY. THE FATHER AND MOTHER CONCEPT IS TOO OFTEN NOT THERE. DISRESPECT FOR THOSE THAT ARE THERE IS PRESENT BECAUSE THEY KNOW HOW THEY GOT TO THIS POINT IN THEIR LIFE. THEY WERE LIKE AN OLD FASHIONED QUILT. EVERY TYPE AND COLOR OF MATERIAL IS USED IN THE MAKING AS THE SEWING PROGRESSES. THERE IS NO PLAN, NO CONTINUITY. MOM AND DAD HAD THE PLAN. OUT OF HOME PLACEMENT AND FOSTER CARE IS GUESSING.

WHY ??? WHY ??? WHY ???

THE CHILDREN'S CODE LAW FOR AMERICA IS GREAT BUT THERE IS NO CONTROL OR OVER SIGHT THAT GUARANTEES ACCOUNTABILITY. THERE IS NO TRACKING SYSTEM THAT TELLS ME WHERE THE YOUTH ARE THAT HAVE BEEN TAKEN FROM THE ARMS OF LOVING AMERICAN PARENTS. WHERE ARE THEY AS TO PHYSICAL, VERBAL, SEXUAL, RACIAL AND MORAL ABUSE? THESE ABUSES HAVE AND ARE SCARRING THESE CHILDREN FOR LIFE. DO WE WANT TO CHANGE AND HEAL THIS EFFECT OR IS THIS THE ULTIMATE GOAL OF THIS PERVERTED SYSTEM? ARE WE TRYING TO BRING FORTH PERFECTION OR SELECTED CORRUPTION AND SELECTED GENOCIDE?

THERE IS NO UNSUPERVISED OR PRIVATE CONVERSATIONS WITH THE CHILDREN TO HEAR THEIR INJUSTICE AND ILLEGAL EXPERIENCES THAT THEY ARE GOING THROUGH IN OUT OF HOME CARE. WHY IS ABUSE REPORTING TO OUTSIDE PERSONS OR AUTHORITIES OFF LIMITS TO HELPLESS CHILDREN CAPTIVES? THESE ARE OUR AMERICAN CHILDREN. HAVE WE JOINED THE CROWD OF THE KILL AMERICAN DREAMS, HOPES, GOALS, AND SUCCESS BY KILLING THESE IDEALS IN THEIR CHILDREN? IT ONLY TAKES ONE PERSON WITH THE SWINE FLU, COLD, MEASLES, OR TUBERCULOS TO INFECT MILLIONS. HOW MANY OF OUR CHILDREN HAVE BEEN INFECTED? HAVE TERRORISTS OR ANTI-AMERICAN IDEALOGY INFECTED THE OUT OF HOME PLACEEMENT AND FOSTER CARE PROGRAMS? FACTS SAY THAT

<u>WHETHER IGNORANTLY OR IN KNOWLEDGE, EVERY EXAMINER OF THE FACTS MUST SAY YES! YES! YES! THEY HAVE!</u>

<u>CHILDREN HAVE TO BECOME FUGITIVES TO LIVE WITH THEIR PARENTS. WHY DO FAMILIES HAVE TO BECOME LAWBREAKERS TO CARE FOR THEIR OWN CHILDREN?</u> THIS MUST CHANGE TODAY! THIS IS A CRISIS AGE IN AMERICA! RULES AND NOT GUIDELNES HAVE BEEN DISPENSED TO ONE THAT KNOW YOU TOOK THEIR PARENTS AWAY AND MADE THEM AN ORPHAN TO GAIN A PAYCHECK FOR A COLD HEARTED MONEY SEEKER. THEY KNOW THAT THESE ARE THE RULES OF A CHILD OPPRESSOR. YOUR INSTRUCTIONS BECOME ORDERS THAT ARE MEANINGLESS TOWARD THE YOUTH. TO THE YOUTH, THESE ORDERS ONLY SERVE YOU AND NOT ME. MY ONLY REWARD IS MY PAYCHECK. I HAVE NO LOVE OR RESPECT FOR YOUR BUSINESS, YOUR COMPANY SUCCESS, OR YOUR CORPORATE IMAGE. I COME EACH DAY WITHOUT GREAT DREAMS, AMBITIONS, OR GOALS. I COME TO GO THROUGH THE RITUAL I HAVE BEEN THROUGH FOR THE LAST FEW YEARS. I WORK, EAT, SLEEP. TOMORROW I GO THROUGH THE RITUAL AGAIN.

MY AMBITION AND GOALS WERE NOT INSPIRED BY FAMILY LOVE BUT BY A FOSTER FAMILY PRISON REWARD. GIVE ME A PAYCHECK AND I WILL GIVE YOU A MEAL. READING A BOOK AND WATCHING THE TV TOGETHER OR PLAYING GAMES AT THE TABLE IS FOR YOUR REAL CHILDREN. IT HAS NOT BEEN FOR ME. I AM ONLY THE FOSTER CHILD, A STRANGER IN YOUR HOME. I AM YOUR

DOLLAR, NOT YOUR SON OR DAUGHTER. YOU SENT ME TO THE PARK SO YOU COULD HAVE A LITTLE PEACE, NOT BECAUSE YOU WANTED ME TO ENJOY MYSELF. I WENT TO THE AFTER SCHOOL GAME ROOM AT THE CENTER EVERY DAY. IT WAS SO I COULD BE OUT OF YOUR HAIR. YOU WERE NOT TRYING TO DEVELOP ME BUT TO GIVE SOMEONE ELSE THE TASK OF RAISING ME FOR A FEW HOURS.

****I AM NOT IGNORANT.

A PERSON THAT IS RAISED WITH A **** YOU TAKE CARE OF ME WHILE I EAT SLEEP, GO TO SCHOOL AND PLAY **** YOU TELL ME WHEN AND WHERE TO DO ALL THESE THINGS DAILY **** THIS PERSON USUALLY BECOMES AN ADULT WITH A WELFARE DEPENDENT MENTALITY. A WAIT ON THE MAILMAN DISEASE. HE IS THE MAN BRINGING THE CHECK. I AM YOUR RESPONSIBILITY, NOT MY OWN. THE ONLY MAJOR MISSING DIFFERENCE I FIND IN THOSE RELEASED INTO SOCIETY FROM THE HUMAN SERVICE CHILDRENS PRISONS AND THOSE RELEASED INTO SOCIETY FROM THE STATE CONTROLLED FELONY PRISONS IS THE ABSENCE OF FELONY CHARGES AMONG MOST OF THE YOUTH PRISON GRADUATES. THE SPIRIT OF DEPENDENCY IS PRETTY NEAR THE SAME.

AMBITION TO GET AHEAD AND EXCELL IN A NORMAL FAMILY STYLE TRADITION IS ALL TOO OFTEN ABSENT FROM THEIR LIVES. WHAT HAS GOVERNMENT CONTROL DONE THROUGH ITS CONTROL OF FAMILY LIFE ON AN UPSCALE EFFORT? THE HUMAN SERVICE CONTROL HAS, TO A GREAT EXTENT HELPED CREATE A

GREATER SENSE OF DEPENDENCY AND URGENCY IN THE MOST VULNERABLE AREA OF AMERICAN YOUTH. AT AN AGE THAT YOUNG MEN AND WOMEN SHOULD BE FIRMING THEIR STAND ON A MEANINGFUL FOUNDATION, THEY ARE SLIPPING AND SLIDING ON A TRANSITION INTO AN UNCERTAIN WORLD.

THEY ARE PLAGUED BY THE KNOWLEDGE THAT THEY WERE RAISED AS STRANGERS AND ORPHANS AND SEPARATED FROM THEIR FAMILIES. THEY GREW UP IN A FOREIGN LAND THAT THEY WERE BORN IN AND YET WERE NOT ALLOWED TO FREELY LIVE IN. THEY WERE RAISED AS LEGAL PRISONERS JUST SHORT OF LEGAL SLAVES. THEY HAD NO VOICE, NO MOTHER'S LOVE, NO FATHER'S PROTECTION AND A SYSTEM THAT ONLY DICTATED ORDER. HOW CAN THERE BE A VALID RUSH TO A CHILD'S PRISON RATHER THAN A CHILD'S FAMILY? ONLY A FOOL THAT HAS NEVER HAD A CHILD COULD CALL SUCH A SYSTEM HONORABLE AND JUST.

FAMILY AND VISITOR MONITERING ISOLATION

A SECURITY PRISON OR JAIL FACILITY HAS ALWAYS CARRIED A SENSE OF DOOM, HOPLESSNESS AND DESPAIR FOR ME. IT ALMOST SEEMS AS THOUGH I MYSELF AM THE PRISONER. TALKING ON A PHONE WHILE LOOKING THROUGH A GLASS SEEMS TO SAY, YOU ARE A DANGEROUS PERSON AND I MUST REMAIN SEPARATED FROM YOU. FOR THE ADULTS, I NEVER CONSIDERED THIS ANYTHING BUT STANDARD PROCEEDURE UNTIL I

SAW IT BEING INSTITUTED IN FOSTER CARE FACILITIES IN COLORADO

A YOUNG MAN WAS ASKED BY HIS CHILDREN CONCERNING HIS EFFORTS TO HAVE THE CHILDREN RETURNED TO HIM. HE HAD JUST LEFT FAMILY COURT. HE WAS QUITE SURPRISED WHEN THE SOCIAL WORKER EXITED FROM HER GLASS VIEWING CAGE AND ADVISED HIM THAT HE WAS NOT TO DISCUSS THEIR SITUATION WITH HIS CHILDREN. ANOTHER OF HIS CHILDREN HAD BEEN PERSUADED, (FORCED), TO WRITE A LETTER STATING THAT HE DID NOT WANT TO GO HOME. AS HE SPOKE TO THE FATHER AND TOLD HIM OF THE PRESSURE PUT ON HIM TO WRITE THE LETTER, THE SOCIAL WORKER AGAIN EXITED FROM HER GLASS CAGE AND REBUKED THE PARENT FOR TALKING TO THE CHILD. THE FATHER WAS FORBIDDEN TO SPEAK TO ANY OF HIS CHILDREN ABOUT ANY ISSUES THEY HAD WHILE IN FOSTER CARE.

TO COMPOUND THIS ISSUE, A MINISTER WAS SPEAKING TO HIS CHILDREN VIA PHONE. HE WAS AND STILL IS A MOTIVATIONAL SPEAKER. AS HE SPOKE TO HIS CHILDREN ABOUT THEIR ABILITY TO SUCCEED AND ADVANCE IN SPITE OF *** THE SOCIAL WORKER INTERRUPTEDTHEPHONECALL.SHE.SEVERELYREBUKED THE MINISTER STATING THAT HE SHOULD CONFESS THAT HE WAS WRONG INSTEAD OF ENCOURAGEING HIS CHILDREN TO BE STRONG, TRUTHFUL AND AN ENCOURAGEMENT TO ONE ANOTHER. HIS PHONE CALLS BECAME (UNAVAILABLE AT THIS TIME),

SIX MONTHS LATER WHEN A LAWYER RELEASED A PART OF THE CASE DOCUMENTS TO HIM, THE PREACHER WAS AMAZED AT THE APPARENT ANGER AT HIS EFFORTS TO ENCOURAGE HIS CHILDREN. HE FOUND THAT ALL OF HIS CALLS WERE MONITERED AND THE REASONS PHONE CALLS WERE DENIED OFTEN DEPENDED UPON THE PRESENT OVERSEER. THE CASE WORKER SAID THAT THE PRISON CALLS ARE MONITERED SO WHY SHOULD HE BE UPSET OVER MONITERING THE CHILDREN'S CALLS.

PERHAPS ONE OF THE MOST DISTURBING THINGS OF ALL WAS THAT A REGULAR REPORT WAS BEING SUBMITTED IN THE PAPERWORK ABOUT HIM, THE FATHER WHEN NO ONE HAD TALKED TO HIM. HIS QUESTION WAS AND STILL IS, <u>HOW CAN A REPORT BE WRITTEN ON A PARENT WEEKLY OR MONTHLY WITHOUT EVER TALKING TO A PARENT</u>? IS THERE SOME TYPE OF TELEPATHIC COMMUNICATION GOING ON? OR IS THIS JUST PLAIN LYING BECAUSE THE CHILDREN WERE IN THE HUMAN RESOURCE CUSTODY? I ANSWERED THE LATTER SUMMARY. THIS WAS JUST PLAIN LYING.

<u>I PERSONALLY CONSIDER THAT A LIER SET IN AUTHORITY IS A VERY DANGEROUS THREAT TO ANY SECURITY INCLUDING GOVERNMENT SECURITY</u>. A LIER WILL OFTEN COVER ANOTHER LIER FOR THE SAKE OF PERSONAL SAFETY. AS OF TODAY, AFTER OVER THIRTY YEARS OF INVOLVEMENT IN SOME TYPE OF CHILD CARE ACTIVITY REGUARLY, I CANNOT RECALL ONE TIME WHEN THE TERM LIER WAS EVER USED IN REFERENCE

TO A SOCIAL WORKER ASSOCIATED WITH PARENTS AND FAMILIES BY ANY AUTHORITY.

NO MATTER HOW BLATANT THE ERRORS WERE, THE TERM LIER WAS NOT USED. FACTS WERE OFTEN HEAVILY TWISTED TO GAIN FREE AUTHORITY TO REMOVE THE SIXTY PERCENT OF CHILDREN NOT SUBSTANTIATED BEYOND A SHADOW OF A DOUBT. IN ADDITION TO TWISTING FOR REMOVAL, TWISTING OR LYING IS OFTEN USED TO RETAIN CUSTODY OF SOME CHILDREN AND TO GAIN OR RETAIN CUSTODY OF THE PARENT BY MAKING THEM A WARD OF THE COURT.

. WHAT IS THE DIFFERENCE BETWEEN TWISTING AND LYING? NONE! IS THIS THE REASON THERE IS SO MUCH LYING AMONG SOME OF THE SOCIAL SERVICE PERSONNEL? <u>DO THEY HAVE THE PERMISSION AND ABILITY TO LIE WITHOUT FACING ANY DISCIPLINE?</u> YOU AND I CAN LIE AND FACE A VIOLATION OF THE LAW CHARGE. WHY ARE THESE GROUPS EXEMPT? REMEMBER, IT IS OUR FAMILIES THAT ARE BEING THREATENED.

17. <u>THE MISSING SPARKPLUG</u>

WHEN A CHILD IS RELEASED FROM CHILDRENS PRISON A BRAND NEW DOOR OPENS FOR THE CHILD. MANY TIMES THEY HAVE NEVER WENT THROUGH A CRISIS WITH A FAMILY BEHIND THEM. WHAT IS A FAMILY CRISIS WHEN YOUR MOTHER IS SICK, YOUR SISTER OR BROTHER FELL AND HURT THEIR SHOULDER? WHAT IS A CRISIS WHEN DAD IS ABOUT TO BE LAID OFF FROM HIS JOB? THEY HAVE ONLY BEEN TO A MALL BECAUSE IT IS TIME TO BUY YOU NEW CLOTHES. THE CHECK CAME TODAY. THEY DON'T KNOW WHAT IT IS LIKE TO HAVE DAD ARRIVE AT SCHOOL EARLY BECAUSE WE HAVE TO GO SEE MARK IN THE HOSPITAL. HE JUST HAD AN ACCIDENT. THEY HAVE NEVER HEARD THE WORDS, HEY MOM WILL YOU BUY ME SOME OF THAT NEW GRAPE CEREAL WHEN YOU GO SHOPPING? I WANT TO TRY IT. THE TV SAID IT IS REAL COOL. WHEN HAVE THEY SAID HEY DAD JERRY IS COMING OVER AFTER SCHOOL? HOW LONG CAN HE STAY TONIGHT? CAN WE USE YOUR FAVORITE CHESS SET TONIGHT OR CAN WE RENT THE SPECIAL WRESTLING MOVIE ON PAY FOR VIEW TV? IT ONLY COST SIX DOLLARS. I WILL PAY YOU WHEN I FINISH CUTTING THE NEIGHBOR'S LAWN ON NEXT SATURDAY. THEY HAVE NEVER HEARD FAMILY INTERACTION. IT HAS ALWAYS BEEN WHAT DOES THE SOCIAL WORKER PERMIT?

CHILDREN WERE NEVER MEANT TO BE RAISED IN AN INSTITUTION. GOD'S PLAN HAS ALWAYS BEEN IN A FAMILY SETTING. TWO PARENTS ARE BETTER THAN ONE AND ONE IS ALWAYS BETTER THAN AN INSTITUTION. GOD ORDAINED THAT A CHILD SHOULD BE RAISED, INSTRUCTED, DIRECTED AND CORRECTED BY A PARENT AND NOT BY A SYSTEM. A SYSTEM TURNS ON AND OFF. A CHILD CAN BE A TORNADO, A RAIN STORM, A SHOWER, A COOL BREEZE, A SUNNY DAY, A BUNDLE OF JOY, OR A BOX OF SADNESS. ONLY A PARENT WITH A FAMILY ATTACHMENT IS ABLE TO GO THROUGH SO MANY MOODS WITH AN UNFAILING, UNWAVERING LOVE. TRAIN UP A CHILD IN THE WAY THAT HE SHOULD GO AND WHEN HE IS OLD HE WILL NOT DEPART FROM IT. PROVERBS 22; 6 WE LOOK FOR TRANSFERENCE OF A PARENTAL SPIRIT OF SIMILAR LOVE, PATIENCE, UNDERSTANDING AND COMMITMENT INTO OUR CHILDREN.

IF OUR CHILDREN ARE RAISED WITH AN ESTRANGED SPIRIT OVER THEM IN AN AUTHORITAVE PERSON, WE CAN EXPECT THE SAME IN OUR CHILDREN. THERE IS A SAYING THAT WAS POPULAR IN MY CHILDHOOD DAYS. MANY OF THE SENIOR CITIZENS WOULD MOCK US IN A JESTING MANNER WITH THE PHRASE, MONKEY SEE, MONKEY DO. AFTER BEING SAVED, I ADOPTED MY IDEA OF THE RELIGIOUS VERSION. WE SHOULD LIVE SO MEN WILL SEE OUR GOOD WORKS AND GLORIFY GOD.

EVERY ADULT IS A VISIBLE EXAMPLE TO SOMEONE. GOD CONSIDERS US AS A LIVELY STONE SET IN A BUILDING. PARENTS HAVE BEEN SET IN THE LAND TO

RAISE OUR CHILDREN IN THE FEAR AND ADMONITION OF THE ETERNAL GOD. THIS IS A PERSONAL CHARGE THAT WAS GIVEN FROM HEAVEN ITSELF. EVERY PARENT HAS RECEIVED THIS CHARGE. NO OTHER PERSON OR NO OTHER SYSTEM IS CAPABLE OF FULFILLING THIS PARENTAL CHARGE. WE ARE CONSIDERED BY GOD TO BE HIS JEWELS. MAL 3; 17 WE ARE THE APPLE OF HIS EYE DEUT 32; 10

GOD'S SPARKPLUG BEGINS BEFORE CONCEPTION. BEFORE YOU WERE BORN. WHILE YOU WERE YET IN YOUR MOTHERS WOMB, I KNEW YOU. WAS GOD'S WORD TO JEREMIAH. JER 1;5 HE HAD ALREADY PUT IN JEREMIAH THE ABILITY AND THE CHARGE TO SPEAK TO THE NATIONS. MUCH OF A BABY'S CHARACTER, ABILITY, AND LIFE DESTINATION ARE DETERMINED WHILE THE CHILD IS STILL IN THE MOTHER'S WOMB. IT IS NOT DECIDED BY A PARENT BUT BY GOD HIMSELF AS HE PLANTS THE SEED OF LIFE WITHIN THE HUMAN BODY. NO ONE UNDERSTANDS THIS MORE THAN A MOTHER THAT HAS LABORED WITH HER CHILD IN THE CHILD'S INFANT YEARS AND A FATHER THAT HAS WATCHED HIS CHILD GROW.

A FATHER WAS ADAMENT ON HIS SON BECOMING A DOCTOR. HIS SON WANTED TO BECOME AN ENGINEER. QUITE BY CHANCE AN INCIDENT OCCURRED THAT PLACED HIS NEIGHBOR'S HOUSE IN DANGER OF SLIDING DOWN A CALIFORNIA HILL DURING THE RAINY SEASON. THE PRE TEEN AGE SON SURVEYED THE SITUATION AND WITHOUT SPENDING A DIME ADJUSTED THE SITUATION

IN A MATTER OF A COUPLE OF HOURS. IN ONE SMALL TIME FRAME, A FATHER REALIZED THAT HIS SON WAS A GENUIS IN ENGINEERING IDEAS. HIS NEIGHBOR HAD BEEN SAVED SEVERAL THOUSAND DOLLARS AND POSSIBLY AVOIDED A NEW HOME PURCHASE. YET MORE SIGNIFICIANT WAS THE FACT THAT THE FATHER KNEW HIS SON AND RECOGNIZED HIS SON'S DREAM AND AMBITIONS. WOULD A FOSTER PARENT FROM WITHIN A FOSTER CARE PRISON HAVE REACTED THE SAME? (SPARKPLUG APPLIED)

A MOTER MET HER HUSBAND AT THE DOOR UPON HIS ARRIVAL HOME FROM WORK. SHE HAD JUST CAME FROM A TEACHERS CONFERENCE AND HAD HEARD THE DISTURBING NEWS THAT HER SON WAS IN THE THIRD GRADE AND COULD NOT READ. THE FATHER SAID THAT IS RUBBISH. HE EXPLAINED TO HIS WIFE THAT HIS OWN IQ WAS ALMOST 180. HE EXPLAINED TO HER THAT HIS SON HAD THE CHARACHTERISTICS OF A GENUIS BUT THE TEACHER PROBABLY DID NOT OR COULD NOT RECOGNIZE IT. HE GAVE HIS WIFE JUST THREE BASIC THINGS TO DO. IN FIVE YEARS HIS SON WAS TAKING COLLEGE COURSES.WOULD A FOSTER PARENT OR THE HUMAN RESOURCE SYSTEM HAVE KNOWN THAT OR WOULD THEY HAVE EVEN BEEN CONCERNED THAT THIS CHILD WAS A GENUIS AND NOT JUST AN ORDINARY AVERAGE KID. GOD ORDAINED THAT A PARENT SHOULD BE A SPARKPLUG IN EVERY HOME. (SPARKPUIG APPLIED)

ONE FATHER HAD A SON THAT WAS PROVING TO BE TOO MUCH FOR HIS TEACHERS AND UNMANAGABLE FOR HIS MOTHER. THE MOTHER NORMALLY HANDLED ALL OF THE SCHOOL RELATED AREAS SO THE FATHER WAS COMPLETELY IGNORANT OF THE HAPPENINGS. WHEN THE MOTHER HAD REACHED HER LIMIT, SHE CONFIDED IN THE FATHER. WITHIN TWO WEEKS THE SON WAS A CHANGED YOUNG MAN. HE GRADUATED AT SIXTEEN YEARS OLD AT THE HEAD OF HIS CLASS. HE WAS IMMEDIATELY HIRED BY ONE OF THE NATIONS LARGEST INSURANCE COMPANIES. HIS CORPORATE PROGRESS WAS OUTSTANDING. WHEN A SCHOOL FAILED, A MOTHER AND FATHER TEAM PRODUCED A PHENOMINAL OUTSTANDING SON. (SPARKPLUG APPLIED)

JEREMIAH WAS A (RELUCTANT SPARKPLUG). HE DID NOT WANT TO BE THE SPOKESMAN FOR A NATION. YET, AT THAT TIME HE HAD THE ONLY TRUE WORD FROM GOD. MANY PARENTS MAY NOT THINK OR BELIEVE IT BUT THEY ARE THE ONLY ONE THAT GOD GAVE THE TRUE PATTERN AND PLAN FOR THEIR PERSONAL CHILDREN'S UPBRINGING AND DEVELOPMENT. FOR ANY PARENT TO WILLINGLY REFUSE TO PROVIDE PROPER GUIDANCE AND UPBRINGING OF THEIR CHILDREN; WHETHER INVOLUNTARY OR VOLUNTARY; IS A REJECTION OF THE PLAN OF THE ETERNAL GOD. IT ALSO CAN CREATE A CURSE FOR BOTH THEMSELVES AND THEIR CHILDREN PER GOD'S WRITTEN WORD. FOR OUR AMERICAN HUMAN SERVICE OR ANY OTHER GROUP, COUNTY, STATE, FEDERAL OR PRIVATE TO CULTIVATE OR SEEK TO EXPAND AN EMERGENCY ROLE NECESSITY TO AN ARBITRARY

TAKE OVER SYSTEM IN ANY WAY IS AN ANTI-GOD MOVE. A SYSTEM THAT REJECTS A PARENT OR DENYS A PARENT HIS GOD GIVEN ROLE IS ANTI-GOD.

A NATION THAT BEGAN IN SEARCH OF RELIGIOUS FREEDOM CANNOT DENY IT'S RELIGIOUS PRINCIPLES WITHOUT STEPPING OFF ITS FOUNDATION. IS THERE ANOTHER FOUNDATION FOR AMERICA TO STAND ON? WHERE CAN WE GO WITHOUT A FATHER AND MOTHER TO GUIDE US? <u>REMEMBER THAT GEORGE WASHINGTON WAS NOT JUST A SON THAT WAS THE FIRST AMERICAN PRESIDENT. HE WAS A HOME SCHOOLED FIRST PRESIDENT. HE LEARNED AT HOME, NOT IN A SYSTEM</u>.

THE DISCIPLINE SECRET

A FEW YEARS AGO I SPENT SEVERAL DAYS IN A MINISTER'S HOME WHILE MINISTERING IN THAT CITY. THIS MINISTER WAS NOTED FOR STANDING FIRM ON THE SPARE THE ROD AND SPOIL THE CHILD BELIEF. THERE WERE FOUR BOYS AND ONE GIRL IN THE HOUSE. ONE OF HIS TRAITS WAS THAT HE NEVER BELIEVED IN RAISING HIS VOICE IN GIVING EITHER INSTRUCTIONS, DISCIPLINE, OR CORRECTION. A RAISED VOICE TOWARD AN ERRING OR DISOBEDIENT CHILD WAS TO THEM AS THOUGH DAD HAD SLAPPED THEM IN THE FACE. HIS CHILDREN ACTUALLY FEARED HIS VERBAL REBUKES MORE THAN ANY PHYSICAL DISCIPLINE HE COULD ADMINISTER.

HE FIRMLY BELIEVED IN PHYSICAL DISCIPLINE AND QUOTED KING SOLOMON OFTEN. HIS FAVORITE VERSE WAS, WITHHOLD NOT CORRECTION FROM THE CHILD, FOR IF THOU BEAT HIM WITH THE ROD HE SHALL NOT DIE. THOU SHALT BEAT HIM WITH THE ROD, AND SHALL DELIVER HIS SOUL FROM HELL. PR 23; 13-14

HIS TEACHING WAS THAT YOU NEVER GIVE UP PHYSICAL DISICIPLINE. SOMETIMES THAT IS THE ONLY WAY A PERSON CAN UNDERSTAND. HOW CAN YOU REASON WITH A CHILD TODDLER THAT WANTS TO PLAY WITH A LIGHT PLUG OR TENDS TO CLIMB A CHAIR TO A SINK, COUNTER, OR STOVE? A SWAT ON THE HAND WITH A FIRM NO IS THE BEST TRAINING THAT IMPARTS AN UNDERSTANDING THAT THIS IS SERIOUS. I MAY NOT BE IN THE KITCHEN WHEN HE SEEKS TO CLIMB A CHAIR. I MAY NOT BE IN THE PLAY ROOM WHEN HE TOYS WITH A LIGHT SWITCH. THIS IS NOT A LEARN IN A DAY SO I TRAIN YOU IN A DAY, EVERY DAY. HIS MESSAGE WAS **** FIRST***** REMEMBER THAT A CHILD IS EMPTY UNTIL YOU FILL HIM. YOU ONLY SPEAK WHEN YOU WANT IT DONE. IF IT IS NOT NECESSARY DON'T PRESENT A DO IT IF YOU WANT TO MESSAGE. HE SAID, I SPEAK SELDOM IN GIVING ORDERS BUT ONLY WHEN I MEAN IT.

SECOND **** NEVER YELL OR SCREAM TO GET IT DONE. THE CHILD WILL INTERPRET THIS AS; IF THEY ARE NOT SCREAMING AT ME IT IS NOT IMPORTANT. THIRD **** NEVER DISICIPLINE IN ANGER. AGAIN THE MESSAGE TO THE CHILD IS THAT IF YOU ARE NOT ANGRY, IT IS NOT IMPORTANT. FOURTH **** YOU MUST RELAY THE

MESSAGE TO THE CHILD THAT EVERY INSTRUCTION OR ORDER THAT I GIVE IS IMPORTANT AND IT MUST BE OBEYED. I AM A PARENT. I AM YOUR CHIEF INSTRUCTOR. IF I WHISPER, IT IS TO BE OBEYED. IF I SPEAK, MY WORDS MUST BE HEARD AND OBEYED. I SPEAK WITH RESPECT BECAUSE EVERY CHILD OR ADULT MUST BE PORTRAYED WITH THE RESPECT OF BOTH THEIR PEERS AND THEIR ELDERS. IF I MUST RAISE MY VOICE IT IS EXTREMELY URGENT. IT IS NOT ANGER OR FRUSTRATION. IT IS SOMETHING THAT MUST BE OR SHOULD HAVE BEEN DONE BY NOW AND YOU MUST HAVE OR MIGHT HAVE MISSED IT. A CHILD USUALLY MIRRORS A PARENT IN ATTITUDE AND MANNERISM. IN TRAINING OURSELVES, WE TRAIN THE CHILD. WE ARE THE BEST AND THE MOST VISIBLE MODELS THEY HAVE IN THIS LIFE.

HE TAUGHT THAT IF WE CAN DISCIPLINE OURSELVES TO PATIENCE IN TEACHING A CHILD, WE CAN HAVE A CHILD WHERE PHYSICAL DISCIPLINE IS ALMOST NON EXISTENT EXCEPT FOR THE MINOR HAND SPANKING AS A NEAR BABY. A PARENT CAN NEVER BE INSTUTIONALIZED BECAUSE NO CHILD IS A ROBOT. EVERY CHILD IS UNPREDICTABLE. SOCIAL SERVICE CAN NEVER BE A PARENT. THEY CAN ONLY SET FORTH PRACTICAL PATTERNS THAT HAVE BEEN SET FORTH BY PARENTS AND HOPE ONE OF THEM FIT THE CHILD IN QUESTION.

ONLY REAL PARENTS UNDERSTAND THAT EVERY NUMBER NINE SHOE IS NOT THE SAME AND EVERY SIZE SEVEN DRESS IS NOT THE SAME CUT. SOME NEED

ADJUSTMENTS THAT ONLY A MOTHER OR FATHER CAN GIVE. A PARENT IS AN ADJUSTER, NOT A CRUSADER. HOW LONG WILL A PARENT WEAR THAT LABEL? UNTIL THE LORD TAKES THEM HOME. <u>WE DO NOT LIVE TO DISCIPLINE. WE LIVE TO GUIDE AND INSTRUCT, TO TRAIN AND DEVELOP, TO PRODUCE A WORLD CHANGING MAN OR WOMAN. DISCIPLINE IS A PART OF MATURING. IT HAS A FACE FOR EVERY PARENT. BUT WITHOUT DISCIPLINE A CHILD CAN BE LIKE A RUNAWAY EIGHTEEN WHEELER TRUCK REAPING HAVOC ON EVERY STREET OR PATH HE OR SHE TAKES.</u>

PRISON DISCIPLINE **** FOSTER CARE CONTROL.

BRETT IS NOW NEARING FIFTY YEARS OLD. HE DID RUN AWAY FROM HIS FOSTER HOME AROUND SIXTEEN YEARS OLD. HIS RUN LANDED HIM IN WASHINGTON STATE WHERE HE WAS ABLE TO DO QUITE WELL FOR A LAD OF SIXTEEN. HE WAS FORTUNATE IN GETTING A STEADY JOB AND HIS OWN LIVING QUARTERS. THE ONE THING THAT STAYED IN HIS MIND WAS; I HAVE TO FIND MY FAMILY. <u>HE RECOUNTED THAT HIS MOTHER HAD VISITED HIM ONCE WHILE HE WAS IN FOSTER CARE. SHE HAD GIVEN HIM A SCARF, A PAIR OF GLOVES AND A CAP. TEARS FILLED HIS EYES AS HE REMEMBERED HOW HE WOULD PUT ON THE GLOVES, THE CAP, AND THE SCARF AT NIGHT AND CRY FOR HOURS CALLING ON HIS MOTHER. THESE WERE THE ONLY THINGS THAT HE HAD THAT REMINDED HIM OF MOTHER EXCEPT HIS MEMORIES.</u>

BEHIND THE HOME THAT BRETT STAYED IN THERE WAS A SMALL HILL. WHEN THE BOYS WERE CORRECTED THEY HAD TO RUN UP AND DOWN THAT HILL UNTIL THEY WERE EXHAUSTED. ANOTHER COUNSELOR WOULD SLAP BOTH OF HIS EARS AT THE SAME TIME. HE FELT HIS HEAD WAS BEING USED LIKE A PANCAKE OR CYMBAL. ONE OF THE FAVORITE EVENTS OF THE COUNSELORS WAS TO PUT BOXING GLOVES ON TWO OFFENDERS AND LET THEM BOX IT OUT. THEY CALLED IT DISCIPLINE BUT WE BOYS CALLED IT THEIR PRIVATE SPORT.

`CHORES WAS COMMON PUNISHMENT. THEY MAY BE ASSIGNED TO DO KITCHEN WORK OR PICK UP PAPER OUTSIDE. WASHING VEHICLES WAS ALWAYS A FAVORITE. DURING HIS DAYS IN A CHILD PRISON SYSTEM BRETT LEARNED THAT IT IS GOOD TO WIN THE OVERSEER'S FAVOR. HE LEARNED HOW TO BE A CON MAN. BRETT LEARNED HOW TO WIN A PERSON'S FAVOR BUT NOT HOW TO REGAIN A PARENT THAT HAD BEEN BARRED.

WE WILL ALWAYS HAVE MEMORIES. THIS IS A COLLECTION FROM AMONG THE LAST THIRTY-FIVE PLUS YEARS. WILL THEY HELP MAKE AMERICA ANY BETTER? I DON'T KNOW. ONLY GOD KNOWS *** YOUR CHILDREN ARE YOUR BLOOD. I WANT EVERY AMERICAN THAT HAS BEEN A VICTEM OF THIS HOME INVASION, FOSTER HOME, OUT OF HOME PLACEMENT, ADOPTION SYSTEM, TO CARRY A PRAYER IN OUR HEARTS. PRAY THAT GOD WILL STIR US AND OUR CHILDREN AS WELL AS OTHERS, TO BE FORGIVING, TO BECOME MEN, WOMEN, BOYS AND GIRLS THAT WILL SET OUR EYES ON THE ETERNAL GOD AND THE SOON RETURN

OF HIS SON JESUS CHRIST. PRAY THAT MULTITUDES WILL SEEK THE GUIDANCE OF HIS SON. PRAY THAT THE SOULS OF THIS NATION AND THE WORLD WILL CHANGE THAT WE MAY MEET JESUS. OUR BLOOD BOND WITH OUR FAMILIES CANNOT BE BROKEN. THE BLOOD OF JESUS SHED FOR US ON CALVARY HAS MADE A BOND WITH US THAT ACCEPT HIM AS OUR LORD AND SAVIOUR. WE BECOME A SON OF THE LIVING GOD. WE RECEIVE PEACE AND JOY IN THIS LIFE AND THE GLORIES OF ETERNAL LIFE WITH JESUS BECOMES OURS TO CLAIM. WE MAY HAVE BEEN A HOSTAGE DOWN HERE BUT WE BECOME A NATION OF KINGS AND PRIESTS WITH CHRIST JESUS OVER THERE. WE CAN TODAY BECOME HIS CHILDREN OF LOVE. ACCEPT JESUS. RECEIVE HIS HOLY SPIRIT. COUNT THE PAST AS SUFFERING IN THE FLESH AS YOU MARCH TOWARD ETERNAL LIFE. KEEP PEACE AND JOY ALIVE IN YOUR HEART. LOOK UPON JESUS AS YOUR EXAMPLE. HE DIED WHILE WALKING IN PERFECT OBEDIENCE TO THE ETERNAL GOD. BIBLICAL WORD BROUGHT A RESURRECTION FROM THE DEAD AND HEAVENLY STATUS AND POWER FOR JESUS CHRIST. THIS HAS A PLACE INCLUDING A THRONE AND HOME FOR YOU AND I FOREVER WITH THE LORD. BE BOLD, BE BRAVE, LET THE WORLD KNOW THAT AT TIMES YOU THOUGHT YOU WERE ALONE. NOW LET YOUR BROTHERS AND SISTERS KNOW THAT THEY ALSO HAVE A PERSON BESIDE THEM. NOT JUST YOU. YOU HAVE BEEN BROTHERS AND SISTERS IN ABUSE IN THIS LIFE. YOU NOW HAVE BROTHERS AND SISTERS IN ABUSE WITH JESUS CHRIST, GOD'S SON AND GOD HIMSELF HAS PROVIDED US A KINGDOM FOREVER. YOU WILL NEVER BE ALONE FOREVER.   PRAISE THE LORD FOREVER.